Fig. 1. Franz Boas, New York City, circa 1910 (*American Philosophical Society*)

THE *FRANZ BOAS* ENIGMA

Ludger Müller-Wille

THE *FRANZ BOAS* ENIGMA
Inuit, Arctic, and Sciences

Foreword by
Rosemary Lévy Zumwalt

Baraka
Books
Montréal

ISBN 978-1-77186-001-7 pbk; 978177186-014-7 epub; 978177186-015-4 pdf; 978177186-016-1 mobi/kindle

Legal Deposit, 1st quarter 2014
Bibliothèque et Archives nationales du Québec
Library and Archives Canada

Published by Baraka Books of Montreal.
6977, rue Lacroix
Montréal, Québec H4E 2V4
Telephone: 514 808-8504
info@barakabooks.com
www.barakabooks.com

Printed and bound in Québec

Library and Archives Canada Cataloguing in Publication

Müller-Wille, Ludger, 1944-, author

The Franz Boas enigma : Inuit, Arctic, and sciences / Ludger
Müller-Wille; foreword by Rosemary Lévy Zumwalt.
Includes bibliographical references and index.
Issued in print and electronic formats.
ISBN 978-1-77186-001-7 (pbk.).—ISBN 978-1-77186-014-7 (epub).—ISBN 978-1-77186-015-4
(pdf).—ISBN 978-1-77186-016-1 (mobi)

1. Boas, Franz, 1858-1942—Knowledge—Arctic regions. 2. Boas, Franz, 1858-1942—
Knowledge—Inuit. 3. Anthropologists—Germany—Biography. 4. Anthropologists—
United States—Biography. I. Title.

GN21.B56M85 2014   301.092   C2014-900088-X
                                           C2014-900089-8

Société
de développement
des entreprises
culturelles
Québec

Baraka Books acknowledges the generous support of its publishing program from the Société de développement des entreprises culturelles du Québec (SODEC) and the Canada Council for the Arts.

Canada Council
for the Arts

We acknowledge the financial support of the Government of Canada, through the National Translation Program for Book Publishing for our translation activities and through the Canada Book Fund (CBF) for our publishing activities.

Trade Distribution & Returns
Canada and the United States
Independent Publishers Group
1-800-888-4741 (IPG1);
orders@ipgbook.com

Table of Contents

List of Figures

Abbreviations

AEM   Archive of the Ethnological Museum, Berlin, Germany
APS   American Philosophical Society, Philadelpia, PA, USA
BT   *Berliner Tageblatt*, daily newspaper, Berlin, Germany
FB   Franz Boas
FBFB Franz Boas Family Papers, APS
FBPP Franz Boas Professional Papers, APS
HUBA Humboldt University Berlin Archive, Berlin, Germany
RLC   Royal Library, Copenhagen, Denmark
Sc   *Science*, magazine, New York, NY, USA

Author's Note

Quotes and photographs from the Franz Boas Family and Professional Papers © American Philosophical Society (Philadelphia, Pennsylvania, USA) are published and reproduced by permission of the American Philosophical Society given on July 23, 2013.

All translations of original quotes, words, designations, and titles of publications and references from German, Danish, and Latin to English by Ludger Müller-Wille.

Cartography, digital image preparation, and cover concept by Ragnar Müller-Wille.

Cover illustrations: Franz Boas demonstrates a seal hunt in a photo studio in Minden, Germany in 1885 (*American Philosophical Society*); Mark Tungilik positioned to harpoon a seal at a breathing hole on the sea ice at Naujaat/Repulse Bay, Northwest Territories [Nunavut], Canada, in November 1973 (Photo: *Ludger Müller-Wille*); sections of maps of Cumberland Sound produced by Franz Boas in 1883-1884 (*Boas 1885h, Plate 1*; Photo: *Ragnar Müller-Wille*).

Dedication

This book is dedicated to the memory of people who contributed to the cultural heritage of Inuit and to the legacy of Franz Boas and who influenced me during my own research with people in the Circumpolar North and on the life and work of Franz Boas.

*To **Aksayuk Etuangat** (1901-1996) and **Allan Angmarlik** (1957-2000), Inummariit (true Inuit) from Pangnirtung (Nunavut) and descendants of Inuit among whom Franz Boas lived in 1883-1884. Both devoted their energy to the survey of Inuit place names in Cumberland Sound on Baffin Island during the summer of 1984 when Linna Weber Müller-Wille, Christine Mason, a former student, and I had the good fortune to work with them collecting contemporary names and, at the same time, reviewing the ones which Boas recorded and mapped with their forebears one hundred years earlier.*

*To **Marius Putjuut Tungilik** (1957-2012), promoter of the integrity of Inuit, their culture, language, and polity; leader and mediator in facing the common trauma of child abuse in residential schools; instrumental contributor to the creation of Nunavut. He was a close and trusted family friend since we met in Naujaat / Repulse Bay in 1973. He gave us insight into Inuit ways of life and philosophy.*

*To **Gerald L. Broce** (1942-2011), dear friend and fellow anthropologist, **Douglas Cole** (1938-1997), committed scholar and colleague, and **Rüdiger Schott** (1927-2012), academic teacher and doctoral advisor. In their own individual ways they shaped my view and assessment of Franz Boas by expressing value and respect to his personal and scientific legacy.*

Foreword

Franz Boas (1858-1942) is heralded as the central figure in the establishment of anthropology in North America. From Columbia University in New York City he trained students who fanned out across the United States to establish or join departments of anthropology, to work in museums or in government agencies. Even a partial list of his students reads like a roster of leading twentieth-century anthropologists: Ruth Benedict (Columbia University), Frederica de Laguna (Bryn Mawr College), Melville Herskovits (Northwestern University), Melville Jacobs (University of Washington), Alfred L. Kroeber and Robert H. Lowie (University of California, Berkeley), Margaret Mead (American Museum of Natural History), Gladys Reichard (Barnard College), Edward Sapir (Chicago and Yale University), and Ruth Underhill (Bureau of Indian Affairs).

In his research and publications, Boas developed concepts and orientations that became central to the discipline of anthropology: the culture concept, cultural relativism, focus on the individual, study of languages, collection of myths and tales as reflection of culture, the study of religion and ritual as central to the values of a culture, and the importance of intensive fieldwork. Boas stressed painstaking data collection as the basis for a scientific study of

Fig. 2. Franz Boas demonstrates a seal hunt on the ice in a photo studio in Minden, Germany, 1885 (*American Philosophical Society;* reproduced in Boas 1888:478)

cultures. He eschewed grand theories, such as nineteenth-century cultural evolutionism, which ranked societies on a scale from barbarism to savagery to civilization. In place of such hierarchical classification, Boas stressed the importance of gathering the detailed components of a culture.

As a fervent believer in the equality of all peoples and a strong proponent of women's rights, Boas advocated for social justice and racial equality. In the 1930s, suffering from ill health and recovering from a heart attack, Boas worked tirelessly in opposition to what he called *"the Nordic nonsense"* of supposed Aryan superiority. He marshalled the data that he had been collecting throughout his professional life on the physical measurement of immigrants and their children to show that physical type is not fixed by supposed racial categories, but changes with improved nutrition and life circumstances. Boas made sure that his voice, as a respected scientist, was heard loudly and clearly. He used the podium to deliver his message both to professional audiences and to the popular press, e.g. his presidential address on *"Race and Progress"* to the American Association of the Advancement of Science (AAAS) in June 1931. He wrote and circulated open letters, the most remarkable and passionate of which was his open letter of March 27, 1933 to His Excellency General Field Marshal Paul von Hindenburg, President of the German Reich (1933a) in response to the imposition of the Enabling Act of March 23, 1933, which transferred legislative power from the Reichstag to the Reich Cabinet headed by Hitler. One of the founders of the Emergency Committee in Aid of Displaced Foreign Scholars (1933-1941), Boas worked exhaustively to place refugees, largely but not exclusively Jewish, in colleges and universities throughout the United

States. As part of this effort, Boas helped to establish the University in Exile at the New School for Social Research in New York City. His article *"Aryans and Non-Aryans"* (1933b, 1934a), translated into five languages and printed on onionskin paper, was passed hand-to-hand throughout Germany, Austria, France, Switzerland, Denmark, Norway, and Sweden.

Claude Lévi-Strauss, who was present at the luncheon when Boas died on December 21, 1942, later reflected that he had witnessed the passing of *"the last of the intellectual giants produced by the nineteenth century."* (1984:9). We tend to recall Franz Boas from this vantage point: a senior, established figure in North American anthropology; as a founding figure, or in the oft-used phrase, the 'founding father' of American anthropology; a giant in the field. Often we forget that when he began to make his mark in the scientific realm he was a young man of great ambition, great promise, and no job prospects. Boas struggled for years to find employment that would allow him *"to work and accomplish something in the tumult of the world."* (APS/ FBFP, letter to Marie Krackowizer, June 4, 1883). Ludger Müller-Wille writing here, as he did earlier in his *Franz Boas among the Inuit of Baffin Island 1883-1884: Journals & Letters* (1998), takes us to this time in the 1880s, when the young Boas began and developed his scientific endeavours and went on his year-long *Erstlingsreise*, his first voyage, to Inuit on Baffin Land in the Arctic in 1883-1884 accompanied by his servant, Wilhelm Weike, whom his father insisted on employing for him.

Increasingly immersed in ethnology but not abandoning geography, Boas charted a course to make his mark through his relentless publications in strategically selected venues.

Three years would pass after he left Baffin Land and sailed for New York City before he would be able to secure employment at *Science* magazine. In the interim, he would spend several months in New York City and Washington; return to Germany to see his family and successfully obtain the *Habilitation*; and finally set sail once again for New York City in July 1886, to journey from there to the Northwest Coast in Canada for his first of many field trips to that region. In January 1887, on his return from the Northwest Coast, Boas walked into the office of *Science*, handed an article, "*The Study of Geography,*" to the editor, N. D. C. Hodges and over dinner with him that same evening was offered the job of assistant editor with a focus on geography. Boas had found his foothold in a new country. Henceforth he would return to Germany only as a visitor to family, friends, and colleagues. For the deeply sentimental man that he was, his heart would continue to be pulled between divided desires, for the home he would make in the United States and the home he so loved in Germany. By examining his German language publications (1883-1894), little known in North America, Ludger Müller-Wille has allowed Franz Boas to speak to us again in his native tongue of "*Inuit, Arctic, and Sciences.*"

Rosemary Lévy Zumwalt
Dahlonega, January 2014
Dean of the College Emerita
Professor Emerita of Anthropology
Agnes Scott College
Decatur, Georgia, U. S. A.

Fig. 3. Franz Boas as a student in Kiel, Germany, circa 1880-1881
(*American Philosophical Society*)

Introduction
Franz Boas, Inuit, Arctic,
and Sciences

> *"... Franz Boas has remained an enigma,*
> *so misunderstood as a person and so often*
> *misrepresented as an anthropologist."*

> William S. Willis, Jr.

In late August 1883, Franz Boas, a twenty-five-year-old German scientist, and his twenty-three-year-old servant Wilhelm Weike landed at Kekerten Island in Tinijjuarvik, Cumberland Sound, on Qikiqtaaluk, Baffin Land, today known as Baffin Island. They would live among the aboriginal Inuit as well as American and Scottish whalers, who had frequented the region since the 1860s.

Boas was about to begin a one-year sojourn to study *"the elementary relationships between Inuit and their Arctic environment."* This undertaking followed in the wake of the first International Polar Year of 1882-83, during which Germany, one of the twelve participating nations, had placed a crew of eleven men at a temporary research station at the northern end of Cumberland Sound. The international consortium of scientists, placed at fourteen locations throughout the polar regions, investigated physical phenomena in synchronized fashion in order to understand the complexity and importance of global climate systems. Boas's choice of location and research themes was certainly influenced by the contemporary scientific atmosphere that strongly encouraged polar research. Another factor was that he wanted to study peoples and their cultures who had very limited contact with Western civilization. It seemed to him that the Inuit of Cumberland Sound matched his expectations despite their sporadic contact with Scottish and American whalers.

Inuit of Cumberland Sound had already been exposed to rapidly encroaching foreign explorers and the demands and rigours of expanding modern industrial whaling since the early nineteenth century. Now in the 1880s they also received international attention from modern Western sciences, and particularly polar sciences. All these many incursions would have an impact on their own future livelihood and culture. This attention would also have an influence on the emergence and advancements of modern natural and social sciences in Europe and North America. These events occurred at the time when, in 1880, Great Britain, the prevailing colonial power, had just transferred its claim of Arctic sovereignty to the Dominion of Canada, established in 1867. Canada only slowly adapted to the challenging task of being an Arctic state. Just one decade after Boas's stay Anglican missionaries reached Baffin Land and within a short time span successfully converted Inuit to the Christian faith. The Canadian government gradually exerted control over its Arctic regions and established a network of institutions and services to bolster its sovereignty. External commercial and industrial interests followed suit and increased over time, extracting resources, some to depletion, throughout the Arctic lands, waters, and ice—the ancestral home of the Inuit.

Boas focussed his research on environmental, geographical, and ethnological questions. His plans were well received and encouraged in scientific circles in Germany. His journalistic reports from the Arctic before the winter and after his return, published by the newspaper *Berliner Tageblatt*, were widely read at home. After he left Baffin Land in early September 1884, spending some time in the United States and then returning to Germany in March 1885, Boas produced a large number of scientific publications about Inuit and the Arctic environment. He published these in Germany, and also, in a few cases, in German newspapers in the United States. In July 1886 he moved permanently to the United States and published mostly in English, but also continued his writings in German.

Boas's German scholarly publications on Inuit and the Arctic have remained largely unknown and neglected in North America. These publications presented his emerging scientific interpretations on his research with Inuit and on the Arctic environment. They provide us two-fold insights: an understanding of the scientific stimuli the young Boas received at German universities and applied during his sojourn in the Arctic, and glimpses into a crucial period of Inuit history dominated by Western colonial expansion into their homeland some one hundred thirty years ago. This historical source in the German language has hitherto not received full attention. On the other hand, Boas's subsequent English publications on Inuit and the Arctic were widely noticed by the scientific community and the public in North America. In fact, they became keystones of

modern Inuit Anthropology, on which successive genera-
tions of students and scholars, including Inuit, would build
their studies into Inuit culture and history. Reviewing
Boas's early German publications will allow a deeper
understanding of his academic background, approach, and
thinking as an emerging multi-disciplinary scientist. He
became an early initiator of systematic studies of Arctic
peoples and emerged later as a central founder of anthropology, which he developed and represented as an academic
discipline at Columbia University in New York City from
the late 1890s to the early 1940s.

There is no doubt that Boas played a pivotal role in the
history of science. Because of his extensive professional contributions to various disciplines and the establishment of
academic institutions and organizations, he is considered
an icon in the emergence and acceptance of science as part
of societal life in North America. His attention to a wide
and diverse range of research problems, his development
and application of exacting methodologies, his extensive
academic activities as a teacher and mentor, his numerous
publications, and his committed engagement in public
actions related to societal issues of race and culture all demonstrate his outstanding achievements and influence. His
cooperation and exchanges with the renowned sociologist
and civil rights activist W. E. B. Du Bois are just two examples of how Boas stimulated the discussions concerning
race, societal changes, and universal rights. He expressed
these views in his commencement speech at Atlanta
University, a black college in Georgia, to which Du Bois
invited him in 1906 (Zumwalt & Willis 2008).

Though we know much about Boas, some aspects of his
personal and intellectual life path have remained an enigma

to this day, and have been a source of extended discussions among scholars of the history of science and anthropology in particular. This relates mainly to his scientific contributions in Germany before his ultimate move to the United States, when he was already a recognized scientist at home holding formal degrees attained within the strict European academic traditions.

In North America, scholars of the history of anthropology have often treated Boas as an American persona. His personal and academic background as a German Jew is usually acknowledged, but not fully explored nor understood. In part, this has been, and still seems to be, a result of linguistic and cultural obstacles that prevent us from appreciating Boas's complete scientific and literary opus and his deep professional and collegial involvement with academia in Germany. During his early academic studies and subsequent research in the Arctic Boas showed wide interests in both natural and social sciences, be it physics, physical and human geography, ethnology, or philosophy. His publications as well as his notes in journals and his correspondence of the time demonstrate that he was accomplished and innovative in all those fields.

Boas used his intensive research on Inuit and the Arctic to publish widely in different venues to reach a broad audience and attain acceptance and recognition by other professional scholars working in similar fields. With boundless energy he carried out these activities, which, over time, led to the emergence of anthropology as part of modern social sciences with Boas as a central proponent developing it into an academic discipline. In his work he recognized the achievements of other colleagues who competed with him in the same emerging fields. It has been stated by some

historians of anthropology that Boas's first research experience with Inuit in the Arctic was a major turning point in
his scientific direction and philosophical position and
prompted him to leave exact science aside and adopt
descriptive science with a concentration on the historical
dimensions of cultures. This transition in Boas's thoughts
and practices was not as straightforward as some historians claim. In fact, Boas did not neglect his earlier scientific
approaches. He continued to integrate spatial, geographical, and environmental aspects and themes, as well as statistical applications, into his later studies and interpretations
of human conditions. Some scholars of Boas's academic
biography have largely overlooked this aspect of his scientific path.

In the broader historical context of the 1880s Boas's
research among Inuit occurred during a politically and
economically charged period of expanding Western discovery and exploration of so-called unknown lands
including the Arctic regions. The aboriginal nations and
peoples who were encountered were perceived as being
'primitive and wild', thus inferior to those of Western civilization. It was also assumed that their cultures, languages,
and livelihoods would soon vanish after contact. It was
considered important to study these cultures to salvage
materials and knowledge for understanding the evolution
of human nature and history as defined by Western science.
In that respect, Western scientific endeavours—as, for
example, expressed by geographical and ethnological
studies—into the human condition globally were very
much part of the unbalanced relationship between
indigenous peoples and the rapidly expanding territorial
interests of Western colonial powers, which disregarded

indigenous forms of sovereignty and autonomous govern-
ance. While studying in Berlin, Boas must certainly have
followed the events of the international Berlin Conference
of 1884-1885, which, by carving up Africa and other regions
into colonial territories, caved in to the demands for col-
onies by the new German Reich. Internally and externally,
Germany propagated strong nationalist and imperialist
policies. Boas disagreed with those attitudes and was highly
critical of those developments. Although Arctic regions
seemed far removed from those events, they were integrated into structures of colonial powers that had reached
northward, subjecting Arctic aboriginal peoples to these
policies and influences.

During his sojourn on Baffin Land Boas carried out an
ambitious and, in the modern sense, interdisciplinary scientific program to investigate human-environmental relations under Arctic conditions. With the assistance of his
servant Wilhelm Weike he studied the environmental conditions by taking measurements and collecting data on climate, tidal fluctuations, ice formations, and topography, the
latter by travelling extensively with Inuit on land, water, and
ice. Through close contacts with Inuit, on whose wisdom,
knowledge, and skills he was completely dependent, he
attained insight into the human condition with respect to
their social, economic, and spatial organization, environmental knowledge, oral history, language, and spirituality.
Boas's perception and image of the Inuit—*Eskimos, Natives,
Savages* in the parlance of the time—had been influenced
and shaped by the prevalent philosophical supposition of
superiority that discounted the idea of universal equality
among all human beings. In short, Western cultures were
viewed as superior versus the 'uncivilized Other'.

Boas's own early writings voiced a similar disposition when he first met Inuit. In that sense he was a *Kind seiner Zeit*, a child of his time, despite having experienced anti-Semitic discrimination and actions as a Jew in Germany. The Jewish community was segregated and singled out based on assumptions about biological descent and religion. For Boas the Arctic experience would heighten the issue of the universal equality of human beings. After a short time with the Inuit he came to the conclusion that they were *"... far from being uncivilized."* This transformation in his philosophical position was certainly caused by his intellectual understanding of Inuit attitudes towards life, which were essentially not different from his own philosophical axiom bound in the Kantian and Western traditions. This paradigm of cultural relativism became one of Boas's major contributions through writing and teaching. By his public advocacy in his later years he dealt with issues around culture, race, and universal equality of humankind fighting fascist and racist ideology manifested by Nazi Germany. The origins of this paradigm are found in Boas's willingness to learn from and accept other human beings and respect cultural differences without judgement.

Ludger Müller-Wille
Saint-Lambert (Québec) Canada, January 2014

1

"... the elementary relationship between land and people ...": Geographical and Ethnological Paradigms

Ever since Franz Boas published his monumental work *The Central Eskimo* (1888), his English writings have been seminal in the expansion of the scientific fields of Cultural Anthropology and Folklore, and more specifically, Arctic Anthropology, Eskimology, Inuit Anthropology, and Inuit Studies in North America and beyond (Krupnik 2014). The 1888 monograph has been quoted over and over again and is often referred to as one of the major starting points of scientific endeavours regarding the peoples in the North American Arctic (Freeman 1984). In this appreciation there has been a neglected dimension of the considerable and important scientific opus that Boas had already published in German during the 1880s. In those publications he had already presented the foundation of his own scientific approach to studying the relationship between Inuit and the Arctic environment.

In the temporal context, Boas was particularly influenced by the geographer Friedrich Ratzel and his concept of *Anthropogeographie*, a neologism that Ratzel coined and which he applied to give proper attention to the human element in the physical environment. It was a novel approach, the *moderne Geographie*, as it was called in the 1880s, to study the interplay and relations between *Mensch* and *Erde/ Umwelt*, humanity and earth/environment (Ratzel 1882). This concept had a considerable impact on Boas's thinking (Speth 1978, 1999). In fact, it became the scientific framework that Boas used, based on his research experience with the Inuit in the Arctic, to develop the *"ecological approach,"* as it would be called later, to study human-environmental relations (Wenzel 1984:90-92, Müller-Wille 1994:30-32, Müller-Wille, ed. 1994:7-11, 1998:11-15).

Boas's German writings and publications between 1883-1894, in which he focussed on Inuit and the Arctic environment are a fascinating and essential source. These works became his defining and lasting contributions to the field that became known as Eskimology in the Danish-Greenlandic tradition and, since the 1970s, as Inuit Studies in Canada and other regions (Études/Inuit/Studies 1977). By the late 1980s these fields were complemented by the emergence of Arctic Social Sciences in a broader sense to accommodate growing interest in research throughout the circumpolar North (Krupnik & Müller-Wille, eds. 2010), more than one hundred years after Boas's early scientific endeavours in the Arctic on Baffin Land, today Qikiqtaaluk / Baffin Island.

In 1885, Boas wrote his first book in German entitled *Baffin-Land* after his stay with the Inuit in 1883-1884. He offered this succinct summary of his early scientific paradigm: *"If the concern is to express the living conditions of human beings with regard to their dependence on the nature of the land, then we need to seek to explain the elementary relationship between land and people very precisely as part of this complex phenomenon."* (Boas 1885h:62). As the eminent anthropologist and social scientist that Boas would later become, he has been and continues to be at the centre of discussions that deal with the history of science and the evolution of cultural anthropology in particular. It is therefore not surprising that scholars have been particularly interested in Boas's early education and academic career in Germany in the 1870s and 1880s, leading to the publication of *The Central Eskimo*, and have analysed his emergence as an influential social scientist and scholar (e.g. Cole 1983, 1999, Cole & Müller-Wille 1984, Dürr et al. 1992, Espagne & Kalinowski 2013, Liss 1995, 1996, Müller-Wille 1983, ed. 2008, Saladin d'Anglure 1984, Stocking 1965, 1996). Yet, despite a number of published biographical assessments and sketches of Boas's life (e.g. Lowie 1947, Willis, Jr. 1972, Liss 1996, Cole 1999, Boas, N. 2004, Zumwalt 2013a, to name but a few), *"... Boas has remained an enigma, so misunderstood as a person and so often misrepresented as an anthropologist,"* as William S. Willis, Jr. pointed out succinctly in 1975 (quoted in Zumwalt & Willis, Jr. 2008:26). It seems that this is still the case more than seventy years after his death on December 21, 1942.

During the 1880s Boas lived and worked in Germany (to June 1883, and again between March 1885 and July 1886), on Baffin Land in the Arctic (June 1883 to September 1884), and in the United States (September 1884 to March 1885 and again as of July 1886 to his death in December 1942). All his life Boas was a consummate and prolific writer publishing constantly in both German and English. Over the span of more than forty years between 1883-1926, he published 87 works of various types and lengths on Inuit and the Arctic: of those, 42 items were in German and 45 in English (see Bibliography for complete list; Müller-Wille 2014). His first publication period between 1883 and 1888 was very intense, with 42 items in German and 27 in English, in all 69 or two thirds of the 87 works. Between 1889 and 1926, his output was 19 publications, one in German and 18 in English.

It is understood that counting titles is just a numerical value and does not provide an adequate assessment of the quality and depth of these publications, which, in Boas's case, varied in length between less than one page and several hundred pages, often with numerous illustrations and maps. Boas's complete bibliography includes 725 titles of publications (711 listed for the period between 1880 and 1943 [Andrews and others 1943] and an additional fourteen unrecorded works found and verified by the author). The opus of publications with titles and content focussed on Inuit and the Arctic represents about twelve percent of his complete bibliography. In many of his other publications Boas referred to the Inuit and the Arctic environment for comparative reasons, presenting particular cases and aspects of ethnography and geography.

These publications represent an extensive body of his work within the realms of geography and ethnology concentrating on the Inuit, their culture and their physical environment. Half of these publications appeared in scientific journals and series, along with one substantial book. The other half consisted of journalistic articles and essays in newspapers and magazines. For obvious reasons the scientific publications in his native German were very much situated within the context of the Central European academic traditions of the time. They were also shaped by the rapidly expanding emergence of *Geographie*, of which *Ethnologie* or *Völkerkunde* was still considered a part. During the second half of the nineteenth century geography became established as a strong institutional academic discipline in Europe and particularly in German universities. It was taught as *Heimatkunde und Erdkunde*, regional (national) and global geography, at practically all levels in the various German school systems.

In order to document and discuss Boas's German publications on Inuit and the Arctic of the 1880s as well as his diaries, letters, and manuscripts published posthumously (Cole 1983, Müller-Wille, ed. 1992, 1994, 1998), it is important to explain both his biographical context and his academic departure and career as they relate to the concepts and the methodologies he applied in his studies and research.

Boas was born on July 9, 1858 into a German Jewish family in Minden (Westphalia) in Germany, where his parents owned a thriving textile store (Boas, N. 2007:1-4). He went to primary school for four years and to the nine-year *Gymnasium*, high school, and received the *Abitur*, matriculation certificate, on February 12, 1877. This date coincided with Charles Darwin's birthday, which, as he said, he would never forget. He studied nine subjects—German, Latin, Greek, French, history, geography, mathematics, physics, and physical education—and obtained grades of *"good"* or *"satisfactory,"* and the highest grade, *"excellent,"* in mathematics. In physical education he excelled as the *Obervorturner*, lead demonstrator in gymnastics, acquiring indispensable skills and constitution for later in life when he would meet physical challenges such as travelling under Arctic conditions (APS/

FBFP). Obtaining the *Abitur* qualified him to study any subject at any German university.

Boas entered university for the summer term of 1877 and attended lectures and seminars in physics, chemistry, mathematics, geography, geology, philosophy, and even, briefly, Russian at the universities in Heidelberg (1877), Bonn (1877-1879), and finally Kiel (1879-1881). He obtained his doctorate—*Dr. phil.* (*Doctor philosophiae*)—in Physics as *Hauptfach* or Major with dissertation, supervised by Gustav Karsten, and *Nebenfächer* or Minors in Geography with Theobald Fischer and in Philosophy with Benno Erdmann. On August 9, 1881 he passed the final examination and received the diploma with *magna cum laude*, the second highest grade, from Albert Ladenburg, the Dean of the Faculty of Philosophy at the *Christian-Albrechts-Universität* at Kiel. His professors, who were also his examiners, judged his dissertation to be a "*specimen diligentiae et acumeninis valde laudabilis*," an example of diligence and very laudable acumen (Boas 1881; APS/FBPP, FBFP).

Despite this academic praise Boas felt himself to be very much at an intellectual crossroads. He had not yet found his intellectual footing nor the focus which would allow him to aim at a career as a university professor. Moreover he was not quite sure that he wanted to pursue such a career. His trepidation certainly stemmed partly from the strong public anti-Semitic agitations by *Judenhetzern*, Jew baiters, as Boas called them and with whom he had negative encounters and altercations in Kiel. In early July 1881, to increase his chances for employment, Boas signed up to take the state examination in geography and philosophy to qualify as a *Gymnasiallehrer*, high school teacher. However, he dropped that plan later that year. He also had ambivalent feelings about his doctoral thesis in physics in which he investigated the changing colour of the water in the Baltic Sea. This he considered to be a *gemäßigtes Opus*, a moderate piece of work (letters to parents, January-July 1881, APS/FBFP). Soon after the doctorate, leaving pure physics completely aside, he ventured first into psychophysics, publishing a number of articles in 1881-1882 (Andrews and others 1943:67) and also began his one-year voluntary military service on October 1, 1881.

At this juncture, Boas turned again to his earlier interests in geography and particularly the polar regions of North America and their *Eingeborenen*, Natives, the *Eskimos*. In 1881-1882, while in the military in Minden, Boas was billeted at his parents' home and found leisure time at night to read and escape the daytime boredom of the barracks and the *Feldlager* or manoeuvre camp (Cole & Müller-Wille 1984:40). On April 4, 1882, he wrote his former professor Fischer that he had decided to leave physics and psychophysics aside to pursue studies in contemporary 'modern geography', as it was called in the early 1880s (APS/FBPP; Cole & Müller-Wille 1984:40-41). On May 14, 1882, anticipating his future direction in research, he mentioned to his sister Hedwig that his only distraction in the army was to read "... *off and on ... something about my Eskimos and make notes afterwards.*" (APS/FBFP; underlined in the original).

Boas's own academic readings were very much spurred by the current waves of scientific efforts in polar science and opportunities offered by the novel International Polar Year, staged in 1882-1883. The German Polar Commission and its scientists participated in this first international scientific program and in its coordinated global network based on synchronized data collection at fixed locations. Germany established and managed research stations on Baffin Land and Labrador in the Arctic and on South Georgia in the sub-Antarctic ocean. In fact, Franz Boas with his *Diener*, servant Wilhelm Weike, was soon headed to test his own assumptions about Arctic societies and their life and environment during a year-long stay among Inuit and a few American and Scottish whalers on Baffin Land in 1883-1884. Between September 1882 and September 1883 the German Polar Commission had maintained a research station at Kingua at the north end of Cumberland Sound, called Tinijjuarvik then and today Kangiqtualuk in Inuktitut (Cole & Müller-Wille 1984:38-41, Müller-Wille, ed. 1998:6-11, 85-90).

In the scientific context of the early 1880s Boas's research foci became a blending of geographical exploration and discovery with cartography, concentrating on *Physiogeographie* and *Anthropogeographie* with hints of ethnography, ethnology, and physical anthropology. By the mid-1880s, after his critical and defining Arctic sojourn, Boas was extensively studying the human-environmental relations as a geographical problem in time and space. Theobald Fischer, with whom he had taken seminars in polar geography, strongly encouraged him in his endeavours. He wrote Boas that "... he [Boas] *could, in fact, advance science significantly by thorough studies of the migrations of the Eskimos and their causes.*" (April 4, 1882, APS/FBPP; Müller-Wille, ed. 1998:12).

By early 1883, before leaving for the North American Arctic, spurred on by Fischer and others, Boas had decided it would be opportune to advance his academic career in the field of geography by obtaining the *Habilitation* after his research with the Inuit. This degree would qualify him as *Privatdozent*, a prerequisite to get a *Ruf*, a call to a chair in a discipline as *Ordinarius / Ordentlicher Professor* or full professor at a German university. In the German university system the *Habilitation* is a postdoctoral degree—*Dr. habil.* (*Doctor habilitatus*)—and the qualification to be appointed to a professorship. The procedure entails the submission of a treatise (*Habilitationsschrift*) and other published works for either internal or external evaluation by several assessors. Once accepted, the *Habilitand* presents a lecture at the *Habilitationskolloquium* before all professorial members of the faculty, who all vote on passing or failing the candidate. The successful candidate is invited to hold the public *Antrittsvorlesung* or *Praelectio*, the inaugural lecture, to obtain the *venia legendi*, the authorization to lecture as a *Privatdozent*, usually an unpaid position (see also Fallon 1976:41-44).

After his interlude in the United States in 1884-1885 Boas would pass the *Habilitation* in Berlin in June 1886. With that success Boas became very much embedded in and influenced by the concepts of *modern geography*, as it was understood in Germany at that time. This was more noticeable in his expanding research, publications, and evolving academic networks than has been generally understood by non-German reading scholars, mainly anthropologists, in North America, including those who analysed Boas's academic and scientific career extensively (Stocking 1965). The geographer William W. Speth (1978, 1999) highlighted Boas's contributions to geography in a broader historic context showing the need "... *to survey the persistence of Boasian anthropogeography in its various expressions and manifestations*," as Kent Mathewson (2002:380) wrote in reviewing Speth's work. In 1947, Robert H. Lowie, one of

Boas's first doctoral students at Columbia University, remarked that *"… for years I failed to grasp how carefully he* [Boas] *took cognizance of geographical factors."* (Lowie 1947:313). In fact, as an example, Boas used cartography as a means to convey the importance of geographical dimension and interpretation. In many publications over the span of his career he included maps, which in almost all cases he had either surveyed, drawn, or designed himself. The visualization of space and spatial organization of both physical and human elements were an integral part of his presentations.

Boas pursued this academic strategy successfully by situating himself firmly in geography, and only later in the 1880s did he move gradually into ethnology, folklore, and anthropology, as he defined this new discipline propagating the Boasian *"science of man"* in the widest sense (Broce 1973:32-35). In 1883, with respect to methods and methodology, he found himself between the prevalent geographical approach of spatial *Entdeckung* or discovery of *uncharted lands* carried out by expeditions, and the novel application of stationary *Feldforschung,* field research as it was already being conducted in polar sciences. He opted clearly for the latter approach, calling his research among the Inuit a *Forschungsreise* or research journey, not an expedition, in the title of his *Baffin-Land* book (Boas 1885h).

Boas's academic development intertwined with his personal growth and with the changes and events he experienced that had an enduring impact during that period of his life and later on (Cole 1999:38-62, 83-104, Boas, N. 2004: 20-40, Lowie 1947, Verne 2004, Bender-Wittmann 2007, Zumwalt 2013a). These factors include:

Fig. 4. The Boas Family in Minden, Germany, circa 1878-80; left to right: Franz Boas, Sophie (mother), Meier (father), sisters Antonie and Hedwig, Aenna is absent (*American Philosophical Society*)

Fig. 5. Franz Boas and Marie Krackowizer in New York City, 1887 (*American Philosophical Society*)

- His increasingly competing loyalties to his family in Germany—his mother Sophie and father Meier, older sister Antonie and younger sisters Hedwig and Aenna— and to Marie Krackowizer in New York City in the United States. He had met Marie Krackowizer first through family connections in Germany in 1881 and was secretly engaged in May 1883 (Boas, N. 2004:290-291,295 and Rabbi Bernhard Brilling [1966] about Franz Boas's ancestors and the background of his Jewish-Westphalian family back to the seventeenth century).

- His life-long *Heimatgefühl* or his sense of linguistic, cultural, philosophical, and geographical identity with Germany, its history and traditions. For example, his *Ex Libris* label showed the view of the *Mindener Dom*, the cathedral, seen across the *Markt*, the market place, from the Boas's family residence and emporium in Minden (Rodekamp 1994:122).

- Obstacles to professional advancement caused by continued discrimination fuelled by prevailing anti-Semitic attitudes in German society and universities while he sought a permanent academic (that is a civil servant) position. Despite the legal emancipation of Jews, non-baptized Jews still had considerable difficulties obtaining such positions in Germany at that time. Boas and his family had experienced anti-Semitic attacks and were well aware of a prevailing public attitude and movement against Jews voiced and supported by prominent academics and Christian clergy in the 1870s and 1880s (Treitschke 1879, Stöcker [1882] 1885; see Mommsen 1880 for strong pro-Jewish statements).

- His serious and consummate commitment to *Wissen und Wissenschaft*, knowledge and science (Lowie

1947:319), which he continued to express in two different cultural and linguistic contexts—in Germany and in the United States—throughout his lifetime.

- His self-defined ambitions, which guided him through all his life. He had expressed his lofty ambitions already in 1875, not yet seventeen years old, in a letter to his older sister Antonie, who was on a visit with relatives in New York City at the time. He noted: "*You wrote in* [your] *letter that I were too ambitious. I tell you, if I shall not really become hugely famous later on, I would not know what I should do. It seems terrible to me to have to spend my life unknown and unnoticed by people. But I am afraid that none of these expectations will ever be fulfilled. I am scared myself of such thirst for glory, but I cannot help it.*" (April 9, 1875, APS/FBFP).

In 1877, Boas had just passed his final high school examination and was headed for university, he pointedly wrote to Antonie about his academic plans: "*In three years I will finish the doctorate and the following year the state exam*ination [to qualify as a high school teacher], *then I will take the Habilitation to become a Privatdozent, that is how I think now.*" (March 18, 1877, APS/FBFP). In fact, he was not far off, except that he would take a deviation to the North American Arctic for one year to conduct research among Inuit.

Boas understood very well that he had to set priorities related to current scientific advances in order to shape his academic career. In the early 1880s he was very much influenced by the prevailing scientific discussions in and around polar sciences and geography (which included *Völkerkunde* or ethnology) at German universities, especially in Berlin. While in the national capital and in other places during

1882 and 1883, he was introduced to many of the most influential German academics of the time. He communicated with Theobald Fischer, Alfred Kirchhoff, Moritz Lindeman, Georg von Neumayer, Friedrich Ratzel, Ferdinand Freiherr von Richthofen, and Hermann Wagner in geography and polar sciences, Adolf Bastian in ethnology and ethnography, Rudolf von Virchow and Ernst Haeckel in physical anthropology, evolution, and ecology, and with Hermann von Helmholtz in physics and statistics. Moreover, he would have liked to take his doctorate with von Helmholtz. This network of academic connections was to become very valuable for his progress and the success in his scientific research in the Arctic. Afterwards it was especially important for his *Habilitation* procedure at the *Friedrich-Wilhelms-Universität* (renamed after the brothers Wilhelm and Alexander Humboldt *Humboldt-Universität* in 1949), which was the required and indispensable stepping stone if he wanted to obtain a professorship.

On April 27, 1883 in a letter to Marie, his fiancée, Boas indicated that the thrust of his intended investigation would be *"... the dependence of the range of peoples' migration upon natural boundaries ..."* and stressed that the expected results were of *"highest significance"* scientifically. He let her know that he was not just an *"adventurous spirit"* or daredevil venturing into the Arctic (Müller-Wille, ed. 1998:38-39). To understand the life of Inuit, he stipulated, he needed to study both human behaviour and natural environment and the interrelationship between them. Boas's first two publications on those subjects before leaving were testimony to his approach. In fact, he staked out his scientific ambitions and let them be known to pertinent academic circles by publishing them. His choice of topics did not come as a surprise, because, for his very first publication, even before finishing his doctoral studies, he had selected the issues around the current changes in the earth's relief. It was placed, probably due to family connections, with a German-American newspaper (Boas 1880) in New York City where, in July 1886, he would settle for life. Did that foretell of later events?

2

Early Geographical Studies, 1881-1883:
Inuit Occupancy in the Arctic

Between late 1881 and early 1883, even during his one-year compulsory military service, Boas was preparing for his individual research projects concerning the Inuit and the physical environment in the North American Arctic. After his discharge by the end of September 1882, he moved to Berlin. There he began to peruse all the available literature, written mainly by British and American explorers and scientists, about the Inuit of the Arctic Archipelago, which had been transferred by Britain to the Dominion of Canada in 1880.

Boas also began to learn Inuktitut, the language spoken by the Inuit on Baffin Land (Dorais 1996:45-52). He used published materials that were available about closely related languages spoken by Inuit in Greenland and Labrador. He also acquired some basic Danish to access the literature on Inuit culture in that language. He contacted scientists, whalers, and administrators in England and Scotland to obtain information about local conditions and permission to stay at a whaling station in Cumberland Sound. There is no record that Boas was in touch with Canadian authorities (Cole & Müller-Wille 1984, Müller-Wille, ed. 1998:4-18,

Cole 1999:63-82, Krupnik & Müller-Wille 2010:378-380). These preparatory efforts resulted in Boas's very first scientific articles on the Inuit (Boas 1883a-b), which he submitted for publication in November 1882. They appeared, each with a coloured fold-out map, in two different issues of the prestigious journal of the *Gesellschaft für Erdkunde zu Berlin* (Society of Earth Science at Berlin) in the first half of 1883, just before he and his servant Wilhelm Weike left Germany for the Arctic in June 1883.

Boas was one of the first scientists of his time to have summarized all available literature sources on Inuit, mainly British. In these two articles he presented and analysed the information systematically and published a cohesive geographical assessment of what was known about Inuit distribution, migrations, and occupancy in the Arctic (Boas 1883a-b; later Ratzel [1887] perused and referenced these and other publications by Boas extensively). Boas discussed the hypothesis that population distribution, migratory movements, types of settlement, travel routes, and use of renewable resources among the Inuit were influenced by temporal fluctuations in the natural conditions of the Arctic environment. He stressed that, generally, movements and resource utilization by human populations are dependent on "*... changes in the climate and ice conditions in those regions*" and that "*... above all ... the distribution of the living areas of the Eskimos is dependent on the favourable nature (or otherwise) of hunting conditions.*" (Boas 1883a:121-122, parenthesis in the original).

It is important to note that Boas clearly pointed out the link between human activities and climatic and other environmental conditions. On the other hand, it should be mentioned that prior to his active research with the Inuit, he approached this deterministic evaluation with a certain scepticism, emphasizing *"... that conclusions of this type cannot be adequately supported by the known facts ..."* (Boas 1883a:119). Based on evidence he gathered during his research later on, Boas unequivocally underlined the direct connection between natural environmental conditions and human behaviour (Boas 1885h:62-90). He confirmed that in the Arctic environment ice conditions, distribution of sea mammals, and other factors affecting hunting potentials had a considerable impact on Inuit settlement patterns, economic activities, and social organization (Boas 1888e:417).

In the first article entitled *Concerning the earlier distribution of the Eskimos in the Arctic American Archipelago* (Boas 1883a), Boas used various sources such as the British Admiralty Chart of 1875 to collate published information on the distribution of Inuit populations for twenty-two different geographical locations between Banks Land and Ellesmere Land and along the western and eastern coast of Greenland. By depicting the geographical expansion of settlements cartographically, he emphasized the issue of the spatial limits of distribution and migrations and the identification of boundaries distinguishing *Völker* or *Stämme*, peoples or tribes, as he referred to the Inuit. Referring to the scant base of reliable information he agreed that *"... the boundaries of distribution of human beings fluctuates ..."* and that *"... boundaries between populations are not solidly defined lines."* (Boas 1883a:121; updated and expanded in Boas 1888e:419-460).

In the second article with the title *Concerning the settlements of the Neitchillik Eskimos* (Boas 1883b), Boas selected a specific Inuit population (*Netsilingmiut*, People of the

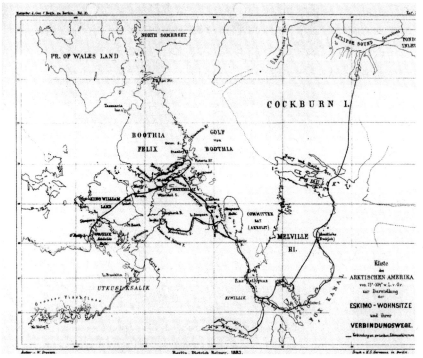

Fig. 6. Settlements and travel corridors of Inuit in Arctic America in the 1880s (*Boas 1883b, Plate 3*. Original size: 21.5x17 cm.)

Land of Seals) to show the importance of the established lines of communications and commonly used, age-old travel routes as indicators of the geographical extent of the use and occupancy of land, water, and ice. The map attached to the article conveyed a clear pattern that the Inuit had developed to utilize and adapt to the physiography of the Arctic landscape. Furthermore, based on quotes from various explorers between 1819 and 1880, in particular William E. Parry and Heinrich Klutschak, Boas referred to the Inuit way of identifying themselves with a defined regional territory by using geographical designations to distinguish themselves from others (Boas 1883b:223).

In these two publications and in another brief report on *Most recent news concerning the Cumberland Sound Eskimos* (Boas 1883c), in which he reviewed the results of the *Howgate* Expedition of 1877-1878 (Kumlien 1879), Boas identified the basic elements of his own research intentions and his plans for the proposed one-year stay in the Arctic in 1883-1884. His aim was to understand the patterns of settlements and migrations as elements of the human-environmental relations under particular natural conditions. Through these early essays Boas also began to grasp the value of the oral transmission of *"tales, traditions, and religious beliefs."* He would later collect these from Inuit as a record of human condition with regard to culture, behaviour, history, nature and space (Boas 1887a, 1888c, 1888e:615ff). Documenting and analysing oral traditions of aboriginal peoples would occupy Boas throughout his life. While carrying out his research with the Inuit on Baffin Land, he learned to be rather flexible in the pursuit of his plans, adapting his studies to local circumstances and to the way of life of the Inuit (Boas 1883d). His journals, letters, and publications are testimony to this constant adaptation. This flexibility to adapt also shaped his research methodology and scientific direction (Cole 1983, Cole & Müller-Wille 1984, Müller-Wille 1994, Müller-Wille, ed. 1994, 1998).

3

Arctic Research and Publicity, 1883-1885: Articles in Germany and the United States

Residing mainly in Berlin in 1882-1883, Boas readied himself both in terms of scientific information and practical arrangements for his prospective year of research among the Inuit. His project was private and independent. He was unemployed at the time and not affiliated with any university or museum, except through informal personal contacts. He knew that it would be difficult to obtain public financial support. However, Boas's research proposal was received favourably by the geographical and polar research community and particularly by the German Polar Commission, which was responsible for Germany's participation in the International Polar Year of 1882-1883. The Commission, chaired by Georg von Neumayer, granted him and his servant Wilhelm Weike generous support in kind (including instruments, equipment, and provisions), as well as free passage on the *Germania*. The schooner had taken the personnel of the German polar research station to Cumberland Sound in September 1882 and was to relieve them in September 1883. In return for this support Boas agreed to share and also publish some of his data with the Commission. In fact, the only case turned out to be about Boas's and Weike's plant collection (Müller-Wille, ed. 1998:85-86).

Leaving Hamburg with the *Germania* on June 20, 1883, Boas and Weike reached Cumberland Sound in late August. They stayed at the Scottish whaling station on Kekerten Island and in Inuit settlements around Cumberland Sound until May 1884 when they crossed the Kingnait Pass to Davis Strait on the eastern coast of Baffin Land. Between May 19 and July 19 they went south and then north along the coast and camped at Kivitung to wait for whalers. On August 28, they boarded a whaling ship at the ice edge, landed briefly farther south, and left Arctic waters on September 1 to sail to St. John's, Newfoundland. From there they took a passenger steamship to Halifax, Nova Scotia, in Canada and continued to New York City in the United States where they arrived on September 21. Weike con-tinued across the Atlantic and reached Minden in early October 1884. Franz Boas hurried to join his fiancée Marie Krackowizer and her family at their retreat called Alma Farm in Bolton Landing in Upstate New York (Boas, N. & Meyer 1999). The following months Boas stayed in New York City and travelled several times to Washington where he conducted library research and made the acquaintance of scientists and Arctic explorers. He finally returned home to Minden in late March 1885 (for more details on the Baffin Land stay see Cole & Müller-Wille 1984, Knötsch 1988; the original diaries of Boas and Weike for 1883-1884 published in English translation in Müller-Wille, ed. 1998, Müller-Wille & Gieseking 2011).

Fig. 7. Franz Boas's planned travel routes on Baffin Land, drafted for Marie
Krackowizer, April 27, 1883 (Sketch: *Franz Boas*; *American Philosophical
Society*)

Fig. 8. Cuxhaven, last German harbour before sailing for Baffin Land,
June 21, 1883 (Sketch: *Franz Boas*; *American Philosophical Society*)

Despite the aid given by the German Polar Commission
and the considerable financial backing by his father and
other relatives, Boas needed additional funds to pay for the
anticipated expenses of his stay in the Arctic. The Boas
family had a number of relatives and extensive business relations in Berlin, particularly within the German Jewish community. These connections provided Boas with information
about possible financial sources with newspapers that were
keen to report on advances in polar exploration. He contacted the *Berliner Tageblatt* or *BT* and, after some negotia-
tions with owner Rudolf Mosse and editor-in-chief Arthur
Levysohn, he signed a contract to serve as *BT*'s special travel
correspondent. The *BT* was founded in 1872 and had emerged
as the first national news corporation in Central Europe.
With this contract the newspaper secured the exclusive
rights to first publication of any news that Boas would send
from the Arctic. By signing up Boas the *BT* also took a delib-
erate step to support polar research and exploration by
keeping these events in the public limelight for the glory of
unser Vaterland, our Fatherland, as stated in the paper's editorial introducing the series (Boas 1883-85, *BT* 3:2).

Such travel reports were quite popular at the time. Newspapers were keen to contract travellers and explorers to write about foreign peoples and lands they encountered during their journeys. This wave of curiosity coincided with the infamous, but lucrative *Völkerschauen* which displayed groups from all continents, referred to as *"savages and exotic peoples,"* in shows and zoos in Europe and North America. The first group of Inuit brought from Labrador to Hamburg, Berlin and other cities in 1880 were among those peoples; all died tragically of smallpox in Europe (Ulrikab 2005). Boas must have read about and was most likely familiar with these shows. In early 1886, he became closely involved with a group of Bella Coola from British Columbia in Canada, who had been brought to the museum in Berlin. As had become the accepted convention at the time, he conducted extensive ethnographic research with these Bella Coola. This was the beginning of his interest in the cultures of the Northwest Coast of Canada (Cole 1999:97). From the record it is not clear whether Boas thought about the ethical concerns related to this particular conduct of research that caused duress to aboriginal peoples in which he also participated (Harper 2000, Pöhl 2008).

The journalistic commission with the *BT* solved most of Boas's financial woes and enabled him to go to the Arctic. Boas's father paid the expenses for his son's invaluable servant and assistant, Weike, who had been in the employment of the Boas family since 1879. Furthermore he vouched for Boas's performance by issuing a matching bond to the *BT* newspaper. Still, Boas was not particularly pleased with the commission, writing his parents on April 3, 1883: *"I am very curious what I will get paid by BT. If it is not much, I promised myself never again to accept such reporting because*

it is horrid work." (APS/FBFP). The agreement called for
Boas to submit three "trial articles" before his departure
and, if they were acceptable and printed, he was to submit
a total of fifteen articles from the Arctic before wintering
and after his return (Boas 1883-85, listed as *BT* 1-18 in the
bibliography; English translation of *BT* 3-18 in Boas 2009).
His "trial articles" (*BT* 1-3) on the status of geography and
polar exploration were published and he was paid separately. Having passed this test, Boas was commissioned for
the articles at 200 *Reichsmark* per piece for a total of 3000
marks paid in advance—a considerable sum at the time.
Boas sent four reports from Baffin Land with two returning
ships, which both had left Cumberland Sound by early
October 1883 (*BT* 4, 6-8). The remaining pieces he submitted between September 1884 and April 1885 (*BT* 9-18),
after he had returned from the Arctic.

The result of these extensive journalistic forays, spread
over a period of almost two years, was an exceptional series
of publications by which Boas reached a large readership
throughout German-speaking Central Europe. The *Berliner
Tageblatt* also syndicated his articles with regional newspapers. Thus Boas became quite well known as a writer,
traveller, and scientist. He popularized geography and
polar sciences and furthered the general knowledge about
Inuit, their culture, and their environment. He also
reported on the expanding external commercial activities,
such as whaling, which had been established in the Arctic
waters of North America during the nineteenth century.

After his arrival in New York City in late September
1884, Boas also intended to publish articles in German and
English in American newspapers. On his behalf his uncle
Abraham Jacobi, widower of Boas's maternal aunt, con-

tacted the editor John Rittig of the Sunday edition of the *New Yorker Staats-Zeitung* to inquire if he would be interested in such articles. Rittig wrote back on October 11, 1884 saying that he could only accept original articles and would not reprint material that had appeared in the *BT.* His newspaper was currently carrying a series on Arctic exploration by Emil Bessels, but he would consider publication later on (letter to Jacobi, APS/FBPP). On January 18, 1885 Boas wrote his parents from Washington that he had proposed an extensive series of ten articles to the *New Yorker Staats-Zeitung* (APS/FBFP). This ambitious plan was only partially accepted by that newspaper, which published only four separate items by Boas, bi-weekly in its Sunday edition between January 18 and March 2, 1885. In those pieces Boas focussed on the European discovery of Cumberland Sound (Boas 1885a) and the annual seasons in the Arctic (Boas 1885b; English translation in Boas 2009:54-66). In a letter to his parents on January 27, 1885 he mentioned that he felt these articles were much better written and more comprehensive than the ones he wrote for the *BT* (APS/FBFP).

Boas's very first English language publication, *A Journey to Cumberland Sound and on the West Shore of Davis Strait*, based on a presentation in New York City in October 1884, appeared in January 1885 (Boas 1884a). Several articles in English followed in the *New York Evening Post, Popular Science Monthly,* and in *Science* (Andrews and others 1943:68-69). Boas also caused a public debate with the American Arctic explorer George W. Melville about the usefulness of reaching the North Pole, which Boas did not consider a priority (letter to Marie, February 11, 1885, APS/FBFP, Boas 1885n-o). Those publications certainly made Boas and his Arctic experiences known to the public in New York City and Washington and later on helped him to obtain his first employment in the United States as an assistant editor with the weekly magazine *Science* in January 1887.

These journalistic activities brought Boas some urgently needed income and made him less dependent on his father, who had continued the financial support of his unemployed academic son. The *Berliner Tageblatt* had paid a handsome sum in advance for proprietary rights to Boas's news stories from the Arctic. In fact, by January 4, 1885, Boas had only submitted thirteen reports (*BT* 4-16) of the fifteen that were commissioned. Boas only solved this problem with the *BT* when he returned to Berlin in late March 1885 and submitted the last two outstanding items (*BT* 17-18).

Boas and the *BT* were already at odds in 1883 when Boas felt that *BT* paid *abscheulich wenig*, outrageously little— only 120 *Reichsmark*—for his trial reports (letter to parents, April 15, 1883, APS/FBFP). On September 7, 1884, Boas announced his return from the Arctic to the *BT* by telegram from St. John's, Newfoundland. At that point, it seems that a *BT* reporter made an indiscreet remark to Boas's father, which Boas took as a claim and misrepresentation by the *BT* that it had equipped him for his stay in the Arctic. Tensions between Boas and the *BT* were also evident in letters he wrote to his parents on September 25 and October 3, 1884. He expressed irritation that he had not yet received the author's copies of all of his articles. He sent a stern complaint to the editor-in-chief of the *BT* (APS/ FBFP, Zumwalt 2013b). Boas was apparently quite impatient, even abrasive, towards his sponsor, because Levysohn, the editor-in-chief, felt obliged to react immediately, stating that he found Boas's message *"disconcerting"* and that he had personally already resolved the situation in print (*BT*

9, editorial note). In his note to Boas on October 14, 1884 Levysohn commented that "... *the matter was not worth the ink that has been squirted over it. So there is no enmity!*" (APS/FBPP).

With this series of newspaper articles Boas had accumulated an extensive publication record on which he drew for various short papers and, in particular, for his two major forthcoming works (Boas 1885h, 1888e), which he had already begun to plan in late 1884. At times he tried to work on these two manuscripts at the same time, one in German and the other in English, but he abandoned that exercise. Writing English still gave him considerable trouble and pain (Cole 1999:90). All twenty-four articles in German, including eighteen in the *Berliner Tageblatt,* four in the *New Yorker Staats-Zeitung,* and two other brief communications (1883d, 1884a), covered specific scientific themes as well as the chronological events during his Arctic sojourn. They are evidence of Boas's keen insight into human and environmental aspects of Arctic regions within the realm of polar science, geography, and ethnology.

Boas had begun his journalistic career by covering the Third German Assembly of Geographers held in Frankfurt in late March 1883. In two of the trial articles submitted to the *Berliner Tageblatt (BT* 1-2), Boas summarized the presentations given on the current state of geography in German universities and schools, discussing issues such as research methods in the *Gelände* or field and the teaching of geography, from local *Heimatkunde,* homeland studies, "*national geography*" to global *Erdkunde,* earth science. The annual assembly convened in the midst of the International Polar Year 1882-1883 devoted much attention to polar science, with the presence of Ratzel and von Neumayer. In his speech on *The Importance of Polar Research to Geography* Ratzel referred to the first meeting of German geographers in 1865 and stressed the crucial shift that had occurred since then. This shift was from exploratory to stationary research in the polar regions. Prominence was given to fixed stations where measurements and experiments, agreed upon by an international scientific organization, were conducted in synchronized fashion (Ratzel 1883). In this way science, and particularly polar science, could be advanced, as stated in a resolution that *"the resumption of polar research is in the interest of science and the* [German] *nation"* (*BT* 1:3). Besides meeting Ratzel and other influential geographers personally, Boas was profoundly influenced by Ratzel's speech, in particular. Ratzel also influenced his approach to his own impending research in the Arctic (Cole & Müller-Wille 1984:41). On May 2, 1883 in a letter to Jacobi in New York, Boas expressed his attachment to geography, *"... virtually for better or worse I must begin with the geographers, because, after all, it is the science that I studied thoroughly."* (APS/FBFP).

In two of the commissioned articles Boas temporarily disregarded the major methodological shift in polar science away from pure geographical exploration, such as reaching the North Pole for *National Glory*, to stationary, carefully designed basic research. In those two articles he delved into the history of exploration in the North American Arctic from its beginnings in the sixteenth century to the early 1880s (*BT* 3, 5; 1885a). To the second of these a brief editorial note added by the *Berliner Tageblatt* said it was published *"... to introduce our readers to the region to which our intrepid traveller* [Boas] *is heading."* (*BT* 5:1).

4

Life with Inuit and Whalers, 1883-1884: *"I am now truly just like a typical Eskimo"*

The contract with the *Berliner Tageblatt* required Boas to send his travel reports at every possible opportunity to Berlin for publication. Before overwintering in isolation in Cumberland Sound, he had three occasions to send reports, letters, and materials: on June 27, 1883 with a fishing boat from Stroma off the northern tip of Scotland; from Cumberland Sound on September 16 with the *Germania*; and on October 3 with the whaling supply ship *Catherine*, which had brought him mail to Baffin Land. The outgoing mail took between five and six weeks to get to Germany. By early October, Boas had managed to file five items published between August 4 and November 25, 1883 (*BT* 4, 6-8). After twelve months on Baffin Land, he reached St. John's, Newfoundland on September 7, 1884 and then New York City on September 21. From St. John's he sent his next report, seven more from New York City, and filed the final two when he returned to Germany in March 1885. This second half of his commissioned reports (*BT* 9-18) appeared between September 28, 1884 and April 27, 1885.

Boas's reports were usually introduced by an editorial note with factual explanations connecting the articles as a series that readers could easily follow. Boas knew very well that he would not be able to see and correct any proofs of his articles before publication. Unfortunately, because the editors and typesetters probably had difficulties in deciphering his handwriting, the published articles contained a number of mistakes and misspellings of names, e. g. *Paquistu* = Pangnirtung (*BT* 12) and *Anamitung* = Anarnitung (*BT* 16). Later on Boas inserted his own corrections by hand in his private copy of the articles (APS/FBPP).

The *Berliner Tageblatt* gave Boas full exposure, presenting its wide readership with his first travel report entitled *Towards the Polar Sea* on the front page of the Saturday issue on September 4, 1883 (*BT* 4). In it Boas related the first section of the sea voyage past Scotland. By happenstance, but as an ominous coincidence, Boas's article shared that front page with the *BT* editorial that reported extensively on *"the end of the anti-Semitic court case"* in Tiÿz-Eßlar (Tisza-Eszlar) in Austro-Hungary in 1882-1883. In that case Jews were falsely accused of murdering a young woman (Jewish Encyclopedia 1906). The clash of news items of the day could not have been more striking and prescient of what was to come.

The published journals and letters, in German and English, by both Boas (Müller-Wille, ed. 1994, 1998; Boas 2007) and Weike (Müller-Wille & Gieseking, eds. 2008, 2011) provide a detailed account for almost every day of the twelve months they lived and worked among the Inuit and the whalers on Baffin Land in 1883-1884. However, those writings were never intended for publication. For his *Nordic*

Travel Reports and Sketches to the *Berliner Tageblatt* Boas obviously drew from his journal entries, rewriting them in a style and language for the general public in the German capital and throughout Germany. However, there was not enough space for Boas to analyse situations and events extensively.

In the first two travel reports (*BT* 4, 6) Boas described the voyage by the *Germania* from Hamburg to the entrance of Cumberland Sound, where they ran into ice and had to cruise for one month before arriving at Kekerten Island and the Scottish whaling station on August 28, 1883. To give their readers a better understanding of the conditions in the North American Arctic the *BT* inserted an article (*BT* 5) Boas had written earlier, in which he described the polar expeditions by Sir John Franklin of Great Britain in 1845-1847 and Charles Francis Hall of the United States in 1871-1873. Both expeditions ended tragically with fatal losses.

In the following item (*BT* 7) Boas gave a vivid account of their arrival in Baffin Land. His first reference to Inuit was about women, whom he called *sonderbare Gestalten*, peculiar creatures, who immediately came on board the *Germania* to visit and trade. He used the term *Eskimos* for Inuit, but introduced in places *Innuit* as their proper name given by themselves. Boas also described his visit to the German polar research station at the north end of Cumberland Sound and the departure of its personnel for Germany. On that short trip he was overwhelmed by the Arctic surroundings and wrote that, *"the appearance of the landscape is truly eerie"* (*BT* 7).

Boas sent the next short report (*BT* 8) and a letter to the Berlin Society of Geographers (Boas 1883d) with the last ship of the season sailing to Scotland, knowing he would now be cut off from the outside world for the next eleven to twelve months. In the report he expressed his frustrations in trying to arrange for his research, including difficulties encountered in his attempt to employ local Inuit to work for him. The *BT* editor was more optimistic, stating in his introduction that this short report was sent *"by our traveller in the ice having a courageous heart."* (*BT* 8).

Boas resumed his reporting after reaching St. John's, Newfoundland, almost one year later. He then briefly summarized the extensive travels he had carried out with Inuit and Wilhelm Weike by boat, on foot, but mainly with dog sleds over ice and snow-bound land (*BT* 9). That article was accompanied by Boas's first published hand-drawn *flüchtige Skizze*, a cursory sketch, based on his own cartographic work. He outlined hitherto unknown details of the coastal regions of southern Baffin Land. The map covered an area of 500 km N-S and 250 km E-W, that is about 125,000 square kilometres, over which Boas and Weike had travelled close to 1,500 km. That map was the precursor to the detailed maps that Boas produced and published later (Boas 1884a, 1885h). It contained nine British place names (including a wrongly assigned Fox Channel, actually Kingnait Fiord), and two Inuit names, Kikkerton (Kekerten) Islands in Cumberland Sound and Nudlung, a cape on Davis Strait (*BT* 9). At the end of his report Boas pointed to his emerging interests in ethnography, stating confidently: *"Because I had acquainted myself fully with the local vernacular, I succeeded in obtaining rich materials concerning tales and religious beliefs as well as customs of the Eskimos."* (*BT* 9:2, Boas 1885b, Part II and *BT* 13, 18; Boas 1887a, 1888c, e; Zumwalt 1982). In a letter on April 28, 1885 to Hinrich Johannes Rink and later on in a publication,

Boas was no longer so certain about his level of competence in Inuktitut (letter to Rink, RLC, Boas 1894a:97; Krupnik & Müller-Wille 2010:380-381).

In the eight subsequent reports between September 28, 1884 and January 4, 1885, two later reports on April 3 and 27, 1885, and another brief communication Boas covered the events and travels on Baffin Land between October 1883 and August 1884 (*BT* 9-18, Boas 1884b). First he discussed the history of European and American whaling and the increasing integration and dependency of Inuit on those imported and imposed activities. In his perhaps hasty judgment he claimed there was a *"... seemingly inexhaustible richness in whales attracting entire fleets and assigning the land an important place in world trade."* (*BT* 10:7). Soon he would revise his assessment by recognizing the major decline and ultimate abandonment of whaling in the Arctic (Boas 1885h:32-33). He observed that the current whaling practices had greatly altered the livelihood, subsistence, and culture of the Inuit (*BT* 11). He continued to give examples of his trips in Cumberland Sound and into Pangnirtung Fiord by boat in the fall (*BT* 12), including the ill-fated march on foot over ice to Anarnitung, when Weike suffered frostbites and was grounded for months at the whaling station. He described the dog sled trips with Inuit to many other places in the Sound (*BT* 14-16) and along the coast of Davis Strait, and finally the brief summer stay in the tent camp at Kivitung from where Boas and Weike left the Arctic (*BT* 17).

For the *BT* readers Boas summed up his experiences and his research with the Inuit in the final sentence of his last *Reisebrief* or travel report: *"The numerous Eskimo tribes of this wide area had become quite familiar to me due to my*

*intimate association with the Natives. Having lived among
them as one of them, I could gain a rather satisfying insight
into their religious beliefs, customs, and mores and collect
something of the immensely rich treasure of tales possessed
by this people who not only struggle with the desolate nature
for their livelihood, but also understand to embellish their
existence by cheerful company, music, and dance."* (BT 17:5).

Fig. 9. Title page of the *Berliner Tageblatt* and a section of the article by Franz
Boas, August 4, 1883 (*Mindener Museum für Geschichte, Landes- und
Volkskunde*, facsimile reprint 2008)

Fig. 10. Franz Boas (right) and a sailor on board the *Germania* off the coast of Baffin Land, August 6, 1883 (Photo: *Wilhelm Weike; American Philosophical Society*)

Fig. 11. The German polar research station at Kingua, Cumberland Sound, Baffin Land, 1882-1883 (*Bundesamt für Seeschifffahrt und Hydrographie*, formerly *Deutsche Seewarte*, Hamburg; file: *German Polar Commission*)

Fig. 12. Franz Boas's journals – June 1883 to September 1884 – in the library of the American Philosophical Society, Philadelphia, Pennsylvania (Photo: *Ludger Müller-Wille*, August 1983)

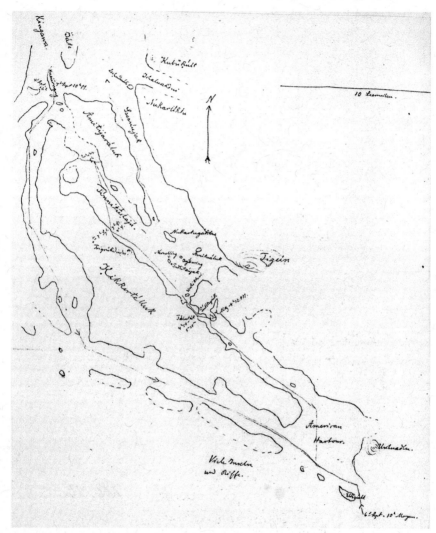

Fig. 13. Franz Boas's first survey map of the northern region of Cumberland Sound with Inuit place names, September 6, 1883 (Sketch: *Franz Boas*; *Bundesamt für Seeschifffahrt und Hydrographie*; original size: 17x 20.5 cm)

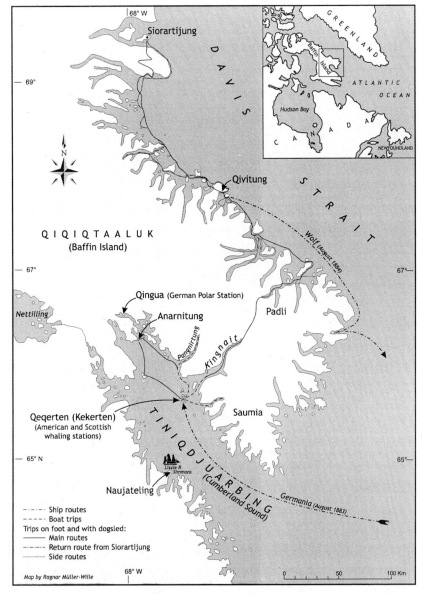

Fig. 14. Travel routes of Franz Boas and Wilhelm Weike on Baffin Land, 1883-1884 (*Boas 1885h, Plate 1*; design and cartography: *Ragnar Müller-Wille*)

Fig. 15. Northward view from the Scottish whaling station toward Kekerten Harbour with (left to right) the *Catherine, Germania,* and *Lizzie P. Simmons,* circa September 13-15, 1883 (Photo: *Franz Boas; American Philosophical Society*)

Fig. 16. Noon break at Ujarasugdjuling, Cumberland Sound, October 16, 1883; Wilhelm Weike (left) and Inuit companions by alphabet, Nachojaschi, Signa, and Utütiak (Photo: *Franz Boas; American Philosophical Society*). This is the first of three plates (Figs 16-18) which Boas succeeded to take of Inuit on Baffin Land.

Fig. 17. Camp at Supivisortung, Cumberland Sound, October 1883; Wilhelm Weike (left) with Nachojaschi, Signa, and Utütiak (Photo: *Franz Boas*; *American Philosophical Society*)

Fig. 18. Nachojaschi, Signa, and Utütiak landing Boas's boat *Marie* through ice floes, Cumberland Sound, October 1883 (Photo: *Franz Boas*; *American Philosophical Society*)

Fig. 19. Wilhelm Weike poses with a dog whip in a photo studio, Minden, Germany, circa 1885 (*American Philosophical Society*)

Fig. 20. Franz Boas imitates seal hunting with a harpoon on the ice in a photo studio, Minden, Germany, 1885 (*American Philosophical Society*; reproduced in Boas 1888:476)

Fig. 21. Mark Tungilik positioned to harpoon seal at the breathing hole on the ice at Naujaat/Repulse Bay, Northwest Territories [Nunavut], November 14, 1973 (Photo: *Ludger Müller-Wille*)

Fig. 22. Hunter, dog team, and igloo on a frozen fiord at Davis Strait, Baffin Land, June 1884 (Sketch: *Franz Boas*; *American Philosophical Society*)

5

Pathways in Geography and Ethnology, 1884-1886: Inuit, Environment, and Beliefs

After his sojourn with the Inuit and whalers, Boas spent close to six months in the United States from September 22, 1884 to March 14, 1885 when he returned to Germany, crossing the Atlantic aboard the passenger steamer *Donau*. He landed in Bremerhaven, where his mother met him, and arrived in his hometown Minden in the early hours of March 26. He had been away for more than twenty-one months. Boas's reasons for not returning immediately to Germany were both personal and professional (Cole 1999:83-104, Boas, N. 2004:72-97).

The stay in the United States allowed him to be with Marie and relatives. He also established personal contacts with recognized scientists and explorers who were active in polar science or in general ethnology and ethnography. The stay enabled him to become familiar with American universities, libraries, museums, professional societies, and government research institutions. He expanded his familiarity of scientific literature and ethnographic collections. This work was

useful to complement his own material, which he intended
to publish as soon as possible in both German and English.
Moreover, at that time, Boas desperately needed to improve
his oral and written skills in English to be able to function
independently of translators and mediators when giving
lectures and writing manuscripts.

During this first sojourn in the United States Boas spent
many weeks in New York City visiting his relatives, acquaint-
ances, and future in-laws. He also went to Washington several times and briefly to New Haven and Groton, Connecticut,
where he interviewed whaling captains and sailors who had
been to the Arctic. His schedule during this period was
gruelling. At the same time, the pressure from his family
and from supportive German colleagues to return to
Germany was increasing considerably.

Returning to Germany and obtaining the *Habilitation*
would not only satisfy his parents, but also would further
his academic standing and opportunities for employment.
His growing connections with scholars nationally and
internationally were becoming an asset that Boas would
foster and cherish all his life. Yet, he was not sure whether
Germany was the best place for his professional career,
given the signs of increased nationalism, which Boas called,
in a letter to his parents on November 7, 1884, the *armselige
Politik der nationalen Sache*, the pathetic politics of the
national cause (APS/FBFP). The nationalistic movement
had become increasingly intense since the establishment
of the Second German Reich in January 1871 after
Germany's victory in the Franco-German War of 1870-1871.
Now *Kaiser* Wilhelm I, King of Prussia, and *Reichskanzler*
or Chancellor Otto von Bismarck were at the helm of the
newly united Reich. Referring to the political position his

former professor Fischer had taken, Boas labelled this movement *eine Schwärmerei für unser neues heiliges deutsches Reich* or an infatuation for our New Holy German Empire (letter to parents, January 8, 1885, APS/FBFP). It was clearly an ideology that Boas could not subscribe to nor condone, as he expressed emphatically in a letter to Marie on January 18, 1885. Moreover, a professorial position in Germany would not satisfy his new vision of his own professional career (APS/FBFP, Zumwalt 2013b). A German professor was a civil servant bound to a set of strict rules to serve the state and the public. Given this situation it is indeed astonishing that Boas did, in the end, take the arduous route to obtain the *Habilitation*. He had committed himself to that academic procedure, however, and intended to go through with it. The successful completion would give him impeccable academic and scientific recognition.

One major concern for Boas was that he had no employment or income in the United States, or in Germany for that matter, except for the occasional payments for journalistic activities, speaking engagements, and fees for publications. He still depended upon his father's generosity to fund his academic and scientific endeavours and dreams. He worked hard to pursue any openings, suggestions, and opportunities in the field, but without any tangible success. Therefore, he needed a double-track strategy that would increase his possibilities of obtaining work either in Germany or in the United States. He hoped such a strategy would increase the potential for making a reasonable choice as to which country would offer the best prospects for settling down, founding a family, and attaining a satisfying and fruitful career.

In the end, after a fifteen-month stay in Germany, he immigrated to the United States in July 1886. He had, in fact, already made that decision with his heart before going to the Arctic, when he expressed his personal feelings in a letter to Marie (May 9, 1883, APS/FBFP). That is not to say that other factors such as the tight academic job market, professional competition and jealousies, political circumstances, and increased anti-Semitic hostilities had no influence in shaping Boas's choice. He had endured all these conditions in Germany (Cole 1999, Verne 2004), and would face them at a later stage in the United States as well (Zumwalt 2013a). Still, Boas was torn between the Old and New World. On January 9, 1885 he wrote Marie from Washington about staying in the United States: *"I want to learn and teach, and I know here is a place for rewarding science."* A few days later, on January 14, he tried to soothe his parents who wanted him home: *"I have promised you not to bind myself here, until I have got to know the German circumstances."* (APS/FBFP).

6

The American Period,
September 1884 - March 1885:
Searching for Scientific Grounding
and Responses

While in the United States in the fall and winter of 1884-1885, Boas was invited by various institutions to speak publicly about his experiences and research with Inuit and whalers in the Arctic. People were very interested in the topic at the time. In June 1884, for example, Adolphus Greely, leader of the Lady Franklin Bay Expedition stationed at Lake Hazen on Ellesmere Island as part of the International Polar Year of 1882-1883, and five men having survived a three-year ordeal were rescued; 19 crew members had died (Guttridge 2000). Back home the Arctic Meeting of the American Geographical Society of New York gave the survivors a large welcome reception on November 21, 1884. Boas attended the meeting and became acquainted with several members of the American community of polar explorers and scientists. His uncle Jacobi and Carl Schurz, both German Forty-Eighters (March Revolution of 1848), looked after Boas's interests, provided connections, and arranged for him to make presentations to scientific societies and institutions, including Columbia College/University, in New York City and in Washington (letter to Antonie, October 29, and to parents, November 22, 1884, APS/FBFP).

The *Deutsche Gesellig-Wissenschaftliche Verein von New York* (German Social-Scientific Association of New York) invited him to give a lecture on November 5th on the *Customs of the Esquimaux* (Boas 1884c). He held his first lecture to an audience of three hundred people and received a handsome fifty-dollar honourarium. His presentation was mentioned quite favourably in the *New York Times*, the first time that Boas's name appeared in that newspaper (letter to parents, October 7 and November 7, 1884, APS/FBFP).

Later in November 1884 Boas gave a formal presentation to the American Geographical Society of New York entitled *A Journey in Cumberland Sound and on the West Shore of Davis Strait in 1883 and 1884* (Boas 1884a), in which he described in detail his travels, surveys, and research on Baffin Land (letter to parents, October 3, 1884, APS/FBFP). Its publication included the first overview map of Boas's precise cartographic surveys on Baffin Land showing additionally, as a comparison, the coastal contours of the latest British Admiralty Chart of 1875. There was a considerable difference in detail and accuracy between the two contours. Boas had been able to survey close to or on the coast using a theodolite to establish and calculate fixed reference bearings to produce the maps (Boas 1885h, Plate I-II).

Boas prepared a third lecture entitled *The Eskimo of Baffin Island* (Boas 1885j), which he gave at the Eighty-Sixth Regular Meeting of the Anthropological Society of Washington on December 2, 1884. In letters to Marie and his parents on November 25, 1884, Boas referred to the occasion as the *Eskimositzung ... mit vier Eskimos* or the Eskimo session with four Eskimos, because the German Emil Bessels and the Americans John Murdoch and Lucien Turner gave speeches as well (APS/FBFP). All four presenters were scientists who had been to the Arctic and worked with Inuit in Greenland, Alaska, and Canada. Boas hoped to collaborate with them in the future and definitely felt that he had arrived among peers.

The speaking engagement in Washington was overshadowed by Boas's persistent difficulties speaking English, which caused him embarrassment. He had engaged Bessels to help correct his English text, and at the meeting the Society's secretary had to read his paper for him. It was particularly difficult for him to participate *ex tempore* in the ensuing discussion of his presentation (Cole 1999:86). There were nonetheless other advances. Boas had joined the modern age and used a typewriter, introducing *getypewritert* for *"typed"* into his own German vernacular (letters to Marie, November 27, 1884 and February 18, 1885; to his parents, November 30, 1884, ASP/FBFP); he and Weike had had a habit of Germanizing Inuktitut words when they lived among the Inuit on Baffin Land (Müller-Wille, ed. 1998:273-276). His proficiency in oral and written English increased gradually and he needed less and less help from Marie, Jacobi, and Bessels to correct his manuscripts (letter to parents, November 22, 1884, APS/FBFP).

Boas continued to orient his publication efforts towards Germany by submitting articles with maps to prominent scholarly journals such as the *Deutsche Geographische Blätter* and *Petermanns Geographische Mitteilungen*. In these articles he expanded the discussion of settlement and migration patterns among the Inuit that he had begun before he went to the Arctic. The first publication focussed on the territorial extension of the seven Inuit *Stämme* or tribes he had identified and which he depicted on the attached map of Baffin Land; the map showed solely Inuit regional ethnic names and place names, and contained only four English names (Boas 1885c, Plate 2). The data were based on his own research and indicated that he had a solid grasp of Inuit geographical names far beyond the areas he had surveyed (Boas1885h:90-95, Plate 1-2). The second paper was a review of the updated map of the Canadian Arctic published by the British Admiralty in 1884; Boas compared that map with his own and with all other known surveys, depicting all in detail on the attached map (Boas 1885d, Plate 19). Boas's exemplary critique of the sources became a hallmark of the high quality of his cartographical and geographical work to which he applied his outstanding mathematical and statistical skills.

In the fall of 1884 Boas laid out an ambitious strategic plan for three major books that would establish him as an authority on both the ethnography and ethnology of the Inuit and the geography of the Arctic. In a letter from Washington, which he visited for the first time, he wrote to his parents on October 10, 1884 that he had a discussion with Otis Tufton Mason, curator of ethnology at the Smithsonian Institution, about publishing his ethnographic material with its Bureau of Ethnology (APS/FBFP). By the end of 1884 John Wesley Powell, the Bureau's director, had accepted his book proposal. Boas began working on the manuscript, which would include ethnographic descriptions of the Inuit, their livelihood, social and religious life, tales and traditions, science and arts, as well as lists of words and geographical names. Powell agreed to include as many illustrations as Boas wanted (letter to parents, December 5, 1884, APS/FBFP). In the end this amounted to close to two hundred illustrations of ethnographic items, sketches, and music scores that Boas had collected. The manuscript in English was almost complete for publication by the end of 1885; however the book was only published a few years later as *The Central Eskimo*, because of administrative and financial issues at the Smithsonian Institution (Boas 1888e). By that time, Boas had issued an inventory list of his donation of Inuit ethnographic items to the Royal Museums in Berlin. In that paper, for the first time in print as far as could be established, he used the term *centrale Eskimos* or Central Eskimos for the Inuit of Baffin Land (1885j:131).

At the same time that Boas began to plan *The Central Eskimo* he renewed his contacts with the German publishing house he had visited in Gotha in April 1883, *Justus Perthes Geographische Anstalt,* publisher of the well-known scientific series *Petermanns Geographische Mitteilungen.* He proposed to its new editor, the geographer and cartographer Alexander Supan, to summarize the geographical and cartographical results of his research on Baffin Land (letter to parents, November 13, 1884, APS/FBFP). By late 1885 Supan offered to print Boas's manuscript as a separate supplementary issue to the series, under a contract with a payment of 986 *Reichsmark*, a substantial sum in the 1880s (letter to parents, January 8 and December 17, 1885, APS/FBFP). Boas began work on this book, which eventually became *Baffin-Land* (Boas 1885h) and his *Habilitationsschrift* the following year.

Boundless energy enabled Boas eventually to write multiple manuscripts in two languages at the same time, be it for newspapers, journals, or publishers. On top of these tasks he also aspired to enter the market for travel books then flourishing in Europe and North America. He thought of approaching the *Berliner Tageblatt* or *F. A. Brockhaus Verlag* in Leipzig and even contemplated using, next to his own, the journals of his servant Weike. This book plan came to naught and never materialized (letter to his parents, April 5, 1886, APS/FBFP; Müller-Wille & Gieseking 2011:230).

7

Return to Germany,
March 1885 - July 1886:
Seeking and Testing Academic
Pursuits in Geography

Arriving in Germany on March 25, 1885 meant that Boas
would be without Marie for the next fifteen months, as she
remained in New York City. On the other hand, he was
again closer to his parents and three sisters. He survived
the overwhelming welcome with flowers and wreaths in
his hometown Minden, where *"... people are making such
a silly fuss over my travels as if I had done something enor-
mous..."* (letter to Marie, March 27, 1885, APS/FBFP). He
returned to Germany with the particular purpose of testing
the academic ground and of establishing, if suitable and
amenable, a basis for a career. For Boas this period became
a whirlwind tour through the complexities and intricacies
of German academic circles and their traditions of formal
hierarchies and structures. In 1810 the German university
system was extensively reformed under the Prussian government and the leadership of Wilhelm von Humboldt
using the newly found university in Berlin as a test case.

Universities became public institutions to conduct research and teach within defined disciplines, curricula, and levels of degrees approved and recognized by the state. This also included the formal career path for a professor, who represented a specific discipline and was a civil servant of the state. In the late nineteenth century this model was partially introduced to the United States, where private institutions were prevalent, and it was used to create state colleges und universities (Fallon 1976).

Boas began his travels throughout Germany within a few days after his arrival. He visited colleagues, universities, and museums in Berlin, Frankfurt am Main, Göttingen, Halle, Hamburg, Kiel, Marburg, Copenhagen in Denmark, and some other places. He stayed briefly in Minden but resided mainly in Berlin, pursuing research and working on manuscripts for publications and the *Habilitation* in physical geography at the *Friedrich-Wilhelms-Universität* at Berlin. For most of this period he was unemployed. Beginning in October 1885, he was hired by Adolf Bastian as an assistant curator for a few months to arrange the North American exhibit at the Ethnological Division of the Royal Museums. This task brought some needed income, which he supplemented by fees for lectures and some publications. Despite all that, he had to rely on his father for larger expenses (letter to parents, June 14, 1886, APS/FBFP).

In Germany, Boas found that he was in great demand to present his research findings about the Inuit and the Arctic environment. He gave a total of eight public lectures at learned societies in various places in 1885-1886, three of which were given in rapid succession. He lectured first at the Fifth *Deutscher Geographentag* or German Assembly of

Geographers in Hamburg on April 11, 1885. The meetings had a strong emphasis on polar research and geography with presentations by Fischer, Ratzel, and von Neumayer. Boas then left Hamburg and went on to Berlin to lecture at the *Berliner Gesellschaft für Anthropologie, Ethnologie und Urgeschichte* on April 15, and finally before the *Gesellschaft für Erdkunde zu Berlin* on May 2. Those three presentations were promptly published, which demonstrated that Boas was very much accepted by the German academic establishment and scientific community (1885e-g).

In his first lecture, called *The Eskimos of Baffin Land*, before an attentive audience of geographers and polar scientists, Boas dealt first with geographical problems by describing the particular characteristics of Arctic topography. For example, he identified correctly the large and unusual land-locked *Nettiling* lake or the Place with Seals as a *Reliktensee*, which meant a lake that was earlier connected with the sea and was now cut off due to post-glacial rebound that caused the remaining seals to be separated from their gene pool to become fresh water seals (Boas 1885e:103, 1885h:50). Second, he stressed that on Baffin Land Inuit "... *exist in a great number of tribes who differ substantially with regard to way of life and customs in a proportionally small surface area. The distribution of these tribes across Baffin Land is definitely dependent on ice conditions.*" (Boas 1885e:103-104). Boas concluded that Inuit located along the coast where extensive land-fast ice allowed easier access to resources such as marine mammals. To his consternation the publisher refused to include the map that he submitted with the article to show these circumstances, however, he was able to adapt the text to make his point (Boas 1885e; letter to mother, August 23, 1885, APS/FBFP).

In that article Boas introduced the terms *Innung* (singular, today *Inuk*) and *Innuit* (plural, *Inuit*) that the Inuit used to describe themselves (Boas 1885e:105, footnote, Boas 1887a:303). However he continued to use *Eskimo* (plural, *Eskimos*), even convincing the Smithsonian Institution to drop the French spelling *Esquimau* (plural, *Esquimaux*) in the title and text of *The Central Eskimo*, where he applied *Eskimo* as both the singular and plural form (Boas 1888e; letter to Marie, November 13, 1885, APS/FBFP). The Algonquian term, *Eskimo*, an external identification by southern neighbours of the Inuit in the North American Northeast, was not replaced in general and academic usage outside Inuit societies until the early 1970s. At that time *Inuit* was commonly adopted into both English and French in Canada, and spread internationally. One might wonder if the authentic term would have been accepted, had Boas used *Inuit* instead and published *The Central Inuit*?

The latter and major part of the Hamburg presentation was dedicated to what Boas called the tale of *Sedna, Göttin der Unterwelt*, Goddess of the Underworld, which he had collected on Baffin Land (Boas 1885e:105-112, *BT* 11, 13, 1885j, 1887b, Zumwalt 1982). By presenting his findings to geographers, he clearly expressed that he saw a connection between the use and appropriation of the environment and oral traditions. He emphasized that the oral record of a people's history reveals the link between geographical and ethnological circumstances. In his view there was an urgent need to collect oral traditions of aboriginal cultures, arguing that peoples like the Inuit and their cultures are vanishing. He wrote: "*Unfortunately, death claims many Eskimos currently and the number of births is very limited, which means that it is only a question of a few decades until this* Völkchen, *this small people, will be extinct; ...* [it] *possesses a wealth of chants and lore which are on par with those of any other nations and offer the study of ethnology plenty of material about their life and customs, which can hand us the key to interesting and important questions for the development of* Wissenschaft or *scientific knowledge"* (Boas 1885e:112; also 1885f:166, 1885h:90, 1887b:623).

Earlier in 1883 and 1884, while Boas was in the Arctic, Leopold Ambronn, deputy leader and astronomer, and Heinrich Abbes, mathematician and physicist, both members of the German polar research station in 1882-1883, had published articles about the Inuit in Cumberland Sound along with anecdotal stories covering their stay and work (Ambronn 1883, Abbes 1884). Abbes published his quite detailed ethnographic sketch in the widely read German geographical magazine *Globus* and, later, in an extended version as part of the official report of the International Polar Year (Abbes 1890). His publications were based on his own observations and information he obtained from Oqaitung and other Inuit as well as the whalers. Abbes included drawings of tools, boats, and snow houses and a list of words in Inuktitut. Oqaitung was hired as a handyman by the Germans and lived with his family next to the station for the whole year. In 1883-1884 he was also employed by Boas for short periods; when Wilhelm Weike suffered severe frostbites in December 1883, Oqaitung and other Inuit saved his life by using their intricate knowledge of dealing with frostbites (Müller-Wille & Gieseking 2011:123-129).

Boas presented his next speech in Berlin in April 1886 before the *Berliner Gesellschaft für Anthropologie, Ethnologie und Urgeschichte,* chaired by its president Rudolf

Virchow. His speech was published verbatim (Boas 1885f, see also 1887a, 1888c). He devoted his talk solely to *The Tales of the Baffin Land Eskimos* explaining some samples in detail, in particular *Sedna*, and describing customs related to birth and death. He also offered a more precise view of his geographical division of Inuit populations in the Canadian Arctic: *Eastern Eskimos* around Hudson Bay, Baffin Land, and Labrador, *Central Eskimos* along the northern continental coast from King Williams Island to Cape Bathurst, and *Western Eskimos* from Mackenzie Valley westwards (Boas 1885f:161; discussion in Boas 1888e:420 with reference to Rink, who included Baffin Land in the area of the *Central Eskimos*, positioned between Coppermine River and Greenland, which Boas [1885i:131] did accept as did Kroeber [1899:266]).

Boas's third lecture at the *Gesellschaft für Erdkunde zu Berlin* gave an exact account of his travels and research on Baffin Land in appreciation of the generous logistical support provided by the German Polar Commission (Boas 1885g). Here he presented his own map to highlight the extent and detail of his geographical and cartographic work (the same map as in Boas 1884a). He also referred to a serious conflict between Inuit and himself over the acquisition of sled dogs. Because Boas intended to travel extensively he needed to acquire sled dogs from local Inuit, for whom dogs were essential for hunting and travelling between settlements. For Boas dogs became indispensable and crucial for the success of his research, thus he became a competitor for a scarce resource (Boas *BT* 14). In addition, he recorded, for the very first time ever on Baffin Land, a ravaging disease that reduced the dog population in 1883. Boas called it *"Diphtheritis"* (1885g:294-295), but most likely it was fox encephalitis (Cole 1999:301). Incited by one particular person, the Inuit blamed the spread of the epidemic on Boas's presence and quest for dogs, whereupon he threatened to discontinue contact with the complainant, who relented under pressure (Müller-Wille, ed. 1998:172). Boas credited the resolution of the situation to the Inuit at the whaling station, who knew him better, and to his own *energetic demeanour towards the main instigator"* (Boas 1885g:295).

Earlier in the fall of 1883 Boas had tried to treat several Inuit, mainly children and women, with medication with little success. There were several deaths clearly caused by introduced diseases (Müller-Wille, ed. 1998:125-127). Some Inuit, who had high expectations in Boas and who called him mistakenly *Doktoraluk* (Big Doctor), probably influenced by the whalers' usage of the term, blamed him for those deaths. Furthermore, Boas also experienced the ultimate limit with Inuit when he wanted to collect skeletons from graves for anthropological studies in Germany. Inuit told him categorically that their graves could absolutely not be touched or disturbed. Boas did not like it, but had to accept it (Müller-Wille, ed. 1998:116).

These episodes provide a glimpse into Boas's personality and his relations with Inuit. Boas's attitude should not be judged by today's strict standards of ethics required in the conduct of scientific research. Such principles were hardly discussed and were not generally a requisite consideration in his time. Boas clearly sensed that there were limits in his relations with the Inuit (for detailed discussion see Pöhl 2008).

During their stay with the Inuit, Boas and Weike bartered with Inuit for ethnographic items such as garments, tools, and ivory toy sculptures, which they brought back to

Germany and kept privately. Boas also assembled a larger collection for the Royal Museums' Ethnological Division, in Berlin, which was under Adolf Bastian's direction. That collection was representative of the material culture of Inuit of that time. In 1885 Boas donated thirty-five items to the museum and published a brief inventory list (AEM files, Boas 1885i). A large part of the original collection was unfortunately lost while being shipped from the Arctic. In 1887 Boas transferred to that collection more items, which he had bought from the Scottish whaler and station manager James Mutch on Kekerten Island (Boas to Bastian, May 24, 1886, AEM). Boas was able to include drawings of forty-six items of the Berlin collection in *The Central Eskimo* (1888e). Most of that collection survived the ravages of World War II. They are now housed by the *Ethnologisches Museum der Staatlichen Museen zu Berlin (Preußischer Kulturbesitz),* as the old Royal Museum of Ethnology is called today.

8

Baffin-Land - Surveys and Inuit Place Names, 1885: Coping with Map Design and Language

After very favourably impressing several influential German academics in both geography and polar science by his lectures in April and May 1885, Boas focussed on finishing his book-length manuscript *Baffin-Land* while residing in Berlin (Boas 1885h). This extensive, all-important book was to contain his original maps redrawn by cartographers and to be published as a supplementary issue of the *Petermanns Mitteilungen* by Justus Perthes Publishers in Gotha by the end of 1885. It became the starting point of his *Habilitation* procedure at the university in Berlin, which he began to pursue during the summer of 1885. This academic process required the submission of publications, including at least one major book-length treatise. From his academic contacts within natural sciences and emerging modern geography, his chosen scientific field, Boas understood that he needed the approval of Heinrich Kiepert, the *Ordinarius* or professor of geography at the *Friedrich-Wilhelms-Universität* in Berlin, in order to be accepted for the *Habilitation*. To succeed he had to over-come one major hurdle—Kiepert, a historical geographer and cartographer, and his annoying and alienating opposition. Kiepert seemed not to agree with nor value Boas's scientific work (see Fig. 23 the original and translated report to Marie, July 21, 1885, APS/FBFP; Cole 1999:89-93).

Later in November 1885, writing to Marie, Boas quoted an overheard statement given by Kiepert: *"Boo, there he* [Boas] *travelled around a bit with one family* [of Eskimos] *and imagines to have achieved goodness knows what. If that should represent ethnological research, then this may become a splendid ethnography! And about that, he wants to write a thick book now!"* (November 30, 1885, APS/FBFP). Well-positioned professors including Dean Wilhelm Scherer of the Faculty of Philosophy gave Boas wise advice and strong support to apply for the *Habilitation* in the designated field of physical geography so as to circumvent the continuing objections by Kiepert, who could block Boas's candidacy altogether. The completion of *Baffin-Land*, his *Habilitationsschrift*, would fulfill the basic requirement to pave the way for him to take the official steps to qualify for a professorship at any Central European university that had a chair in geography (HUBA, *Habilitation* File Franz Boas, 1886).

At this stage Boas was accustomed to producing manuscript after manuscript rapidly, thus writing a lengthier text did not seem to pose a major problem for him. By late August 1885 he had already returned the corrected proofs to the publisher. His major remaining concerns were the design and production of the maps based on his own surveys and calculations and the innovative approach of having the hundreds of original place names in Inuktitut printed on the maps in a consistent orthography. He had obtained the names from Inuit experts.

The cartographic work and the map design took time and became quite tedious. A constant back and forth was required between Boas and the publisher's designers and draughtsmen to ensure accuracy. Boas had to recalculate most of the bearings and positions he had taken during his field surveys on Baffin Land. He was also dissatisfied with the type-setters and, despite his efforts, some omissions and orthographic mistakes unfortunately remained in the final print (letter to his father, August 28, 1885, APS/FBFP; Boas 1885h:42, Footnote 3). The publisher evidently found the map production quite complex and expensive and suggested excluding some of the coloured inset maps (letter to Marie, October 9, 1885, APS/FBFP). Boas did not agree. He pressured and convinced the editor, who ended up publishing all the maps.

The linguistic matters concerning the orthographic representation of Inuktitut was an even more serious task. Boas had extensive linguistic experiences. In addition to his native German, in which he excelled in speech and prose, he had learned Latin, Greek, and French in school. He acquired some basic Hebrew as well and had private tutoring in English, which later became his second language. At the university in Heidelberg he took a beginner's course in Russian. In preparation for his Arctic work, he had endeavoured to learn as much Danish as he could, as it was indispensable for reading the relevant literature on the Inuit in Greenland. To prepare him for his research with the Inuit, he acquired the basics in Inuit dialects spoken in Greenland and Labrador by using materials published foremost by German and Danish speaking Moravian

Berlin West, 26a Kanonier Street, Third Floor
July 21, 1885

The visit to Kiepert's
or
The amiable Professor
The door bell rings. Mrs Kiepert opens; then exclaims:
  Heinrich, somebody is here. [to visitor] *My Heinrich is sleeping a bit.*
  Visitor, commonly known as Franz, introduces himself.
  Kiepert says: Yes, Kirchhoff wrote me about you, but I am a historical geographer. I understand nothing of your matters, Helmholtz needs to look after this.
  Ego: I am a geographer and intend to submit the results of my travels.
  K.: So, I do not have time now, first I need to take a rest, then there is the geologists' assembly here, then I must go to London. I do not have time for anything before the end of October. Also, I do not want to have anything to do with modern geography. It is surely Bastian's task to evaluate your treatise.
  I most humbly request his opinion concerning the habilitation.
  K.: Yes, this field is not yet developed, and possibly you could get something to do eventually. Naturally, you would not have any students during the first years. I cannot tell you anything now, we will talk about that in October.

  I take my leave.
  Adieu.

Fig. 23. Visit to Professor Heinrich Kiepert - hand-written letter by Franz Boas sent to his fiancée Marie Krackowizer from Berlin to New York City, July 21, 1885 (*American Philosophical Society*; English translation by Ludger Müller-Wille and Linna Weber Müller-Wille).

Berlin W, Kanonierstr 26 a II
21 VII 85.

Der Besuch bei Kiepert
oder
Der liebenswürdige Professor.

Erster Akt. Frau Kiepert öffnet, zu dem

Heinrich hier ist Jemand (zum Besuch) Mein Heinrich
schläft etwas.

Darauf, ruft: Franz stellt mich vor etc.

Kiepert sagt, Ja, Hirschoff hat mir über Sie geschrieben,
aber ich bin historischer Geograph. Von Ihren Sachen verstehe ich
nichts, das muss Helmholtz machen.

Ich: Ich bin Geograph und beabsichtige meine Reiseergebnisse
vorzulegen.

K. Ja, ich habe jetzt keine Zeit, erst will ich mich erholen,
dann ist die Geologenversammlung, dann muss ich nach Leiden.
Vor Ende October habe ich gar keine Zeit. Ich will auch
nichts mit modernen Geographen zu thun haben, das ist doch

Darum Sache, Ihre Schaft zu beurtheilen.

Ich bitte unterthänigst um eine Ansicht als Habilitationen.

K: Ja, das Feld ist ja ganz unangebaut, und vielleicht können Sie
mit der Zeit was zu thun kriegen. Natürlich haben Sie in den ersten
Jahren keine Zuhörer. Jetzt kann ich Ihnen nichts sagen,
nur wollen im October darüber sprechen.

Empfehle mich.
Adieu.

missionaries. Nonetheless, as anybody else in such a situation, Boas faced significant linguistic challenges to learn the Baffin Land variety of Inuktitut orally since there was very little substantial written material he could rely on. He learned directly with the Inuit constantly conversing, recording, and documenting vocabulary, grammar, place names, tales, and songs. Thus he was the first outsider who documented the Inuktitut spoken on southern Baffin Land at that time (Boas 1885k [RLC], 1894a). James Mutch, who, at that time, had already lived on Kekerten Island for close to twenty years and had an Inuit wife, was fully immersed and fluent in Inuktitut. He assisted Boas extensively by translating and sharing his knowledge of Inuit culture, language, customs, and beliefs (Müller-Wille, ed. 1998:107, 111; Harper 2008).

Despite all his linguistic efforts, Boas recognized his deficiencies in Inuktitut and tried his best to overcome these challenges by getting advice from people more proficient in Inuit languages, such as James Mutch and Hinrich Johannes Rink in Copenhagen (Boas 1894a:97; Müller-Wille, ed. 1998:160, Harper 2008:56-57, Krupnik & Müller-Wille 2010:378-380). For publishing original texts, lists of words, and personal and geographic names in Inuktitut he had to make sure that he presented their spellings correctly and consistently according to a set standard. Already before his sojourn with the Inuit he had contacted Rink, a scholar in Greenlandic culture and language (Müller-Wille, ed. 1998:8). Boas renewed the correspondence in December 1884, and in late April 1885 he sent Rink a handwritten copy of all the Inuit tales and songs he had collected, in both Inuktitut and German translation (Boas to Rink, April 28, 1885, RLC; Boas 1885k). At Boas's initiative this collection comprising fifty-one tales, songs, and fables was referenced as an unpublished manuscript with the title given in English and the indication that Boas would publish materials on Inuktitut grammar, syntax, and vocabulary (Pilling 1887:12; Boas 1984a). In his letter to Rink, Boas had asked him to check the material and make revisions, which Boas eventually used for *The Central Eskimo* (Boas 1888e:561-658). To speed up the process, particularly with respect to Inuit place names, Boas travelled to Copenhagen for a few days in mid-June 1885 to work with Rink.

It was an intensive, but rather uneasy visit for Boas. Rink, who was fluent in Greenlandic and also a native speaker of German, told Boas that some of the Inuit tales he had written down as *Urtext* or original and authentic text of Inuit oral literature and translated into German were not fully comprehensible and, in his estimation, could not be used linguistically. As far as can be established, these texts collected by Boas were among the first Inuit tales from Baffin Land that Rink had seen and reviewed. Understandably, Boas was disappointed and discouraged by Rink's assessment. Writing to Marie from Copenhagen, Boas commented that he was well received by the Danish colleagues, who spoke German with him, and that he regretted not knowing more conversational Danish. Of Rink he wrote: *"After all I find Old Rink very dull."* (June 12-15, 1885, APS/FBFP). Yet he needed and was dependent upon Rink's advice. In addition to the tales, Rink checked all place names carefully and revised the list according to the standardized orthography developed by Samuel Kleinschmidt for use in Greenland. He also corrected and added to the German translations. Boas acknowledged and appreciated Rink's collegial cooperation very much (Boas

1885h:90). Shortly after the visit Rink asked Boas a favour to review an English language manuscript he had written for the Smithsonian Institution; Boas was glad to oblige (Rink to Boas, August 3, 1885; Boas to his mother, August 23, 1885, APS/FBFP).

In fact, over the next few years, Rink became Boas's most important and indispensable mentor in matters of Inuit culture and language. This was similar to Boas's relation with Mutch who, in a different way, provided him constantly with more new materials directly obtained from Inuit on Baffin Land, but in English translation, which Boas used for his publications. Boas gave Mutch full credit by listing his name as one of the contributors to one of his major publications (letter to Marie, November 13, 1885, APS/FBFP, Boas 1901, 1907). Mutch was also an author of an article on whaling in the *Boas Anniversary Volume* of 1906 (Laufer 1906, Mutch 1906, Harper 2008). Boas and Rink continued their correspondence, published together, and reviewed and showed interest in each other's work and publications until Rink's death in December 1893 (Boas 1886b, 1894a:97, Rink 1890, Rink & Boas 1889).

9

Vagaries of Arctic Geography, 1886: Landscapes and Human Occupancy

On December 17, 1885 Boas was quite relieved when he received the first copies of the much-anticipated book *Baffin-Land*, issued on time by the publisher. The honourarium of 986 *Reichsmark* was promptly paid out easing Boas's financial woes. He nonetheless found fault with the large fold-out map (Boas 1885h, Plate 1) because he was not pleased at all with the cartographic representation of the physical terrain. He was aware that Kiepert criticised his research, as he wrote to Marie *".... some people have attacked* [me] *in a despicable manner"* (December 17, 1885, APS/ FBFP). However, Boas only had to wait a short while for praise of his scientific achievements. An immediate and positive reaction came from Theobald Fischer, his committed mentor and strongest supporter, who stated, as Boas wrote to Marie, that this book was *"an excellent* Habilitationsschrift"* (January 5, 1886, APS/FBFP). Clearly Boas had made a major contribution to the advancement of modern geography. More favourable reviews would follow soon in the relevant scientific journals.

On the frontispiece of his book, Boas showed his deep-felt appreciation for having received guiding mentorship by dedicating his work to *Herrn Dr Emil Bessels, the bold polar traveller and indefatigable promoter of Arctic research with amicable disposition by the author* (Boas 1885h). Boas had met Bessels at the Smithsonian Institution in Washington in October 1884 and received highly valued advice and friendly cooperation.

Baffin-Land.

Geographische Ergebnisse

einer

in den Jahren 1883 und 1884 ausgeführten Forschungsreise.

Von

Dr. Franz Boas.

Mit zwei Karten und neun Skizzen im Text.

(ERGÄNZUNGSHEFT No. 80 ZU „PETERMANNS MITTEILUNGEN".)

GOTHA: JUSTUS PERTHES.
1885.

Fig. 24. *Baffin-Land* - the title page of Franz Boas's first major German publication, 1885 (*Boas 1885h*)

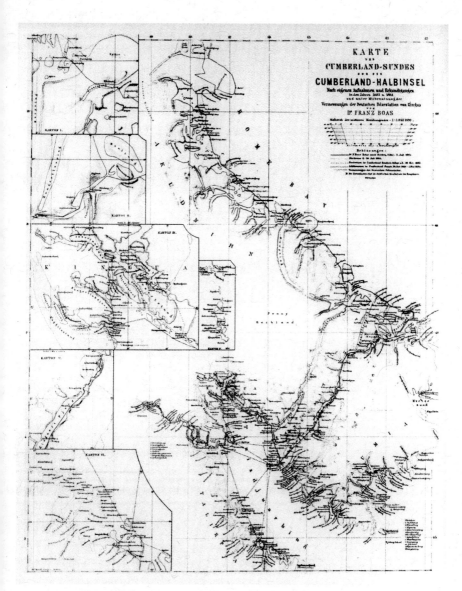

Fig. 25. Map of Cumberland Sound and Cumberland Peninsula, Baffin Land,
1883-1884 (Design and cartography: *Franz Boas*; *Boas 1885h, Plate 1*.
Original size: 41x52 cm.)

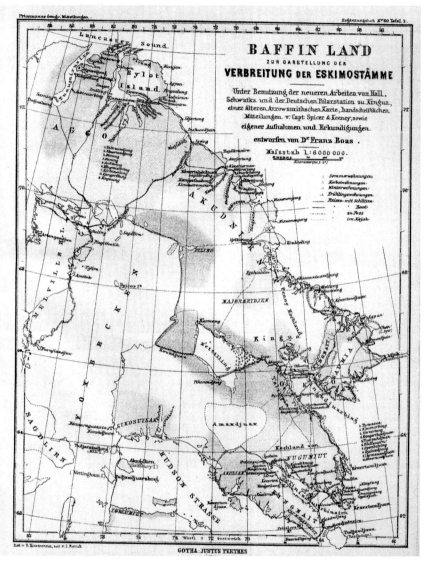

Fig. 26. Map of Baffin Land and the distribution of Inuit in the 1880s (Design and cartography: *Franz Boas*; *Boas 1885h, Plate 2.* Original size: 18x23.5 cm.)

Boas had structured his hundred-page double column *Baffin-Land* book (Boas 1885h) according to the prevailing premises of contemporary modern geographical studies, which had the investigation of 'unknown' regions as their central focus. He divided his book into four chapters with several maps and added two extensive appendices. Appendix 1 contains the list of Inuit place names with German translations and synonyms of names given by explorers and whalers. All names are included on the maps (Boas 1885h:90-93, Plate 1-2). Appendix 2 includes astronomical observations of sixty-one locations and a list of his more important trips in southern Baffin Land for 1883-1884 (Boas 1885h:95-100). To write *Baffin-Land* Boas relied heavily on his journals, notes, and letters; these were published a century later (Cole 1983, Müller-Wille, ed. 1994, 1998).

In the first chapter Boas presented a detailed *Travel Report* (Boas 1885h:1-22), in essence a logbook, in which he mentioned and explained chronologically all routes, places, events, conditions, practical matters, research logistics, methods, seascapes, landscapes, and people. With respect to planning his travels, he stressed the fact that he always asked local Inuit for advice when preparing and leaving on any survey trip, *"... by letting the Eskimos draw the configuration of the area to be surveyed at large scale* [on carton paper], *an art in which almost all developed great skills."* (Boas 1885h:23). He gave particular recognition by name to two Inuit, Signa and Oqaitung, whom he hired as guides, and to Weike, his indispensable servant and assistant. He continued his habit of consistently using Inuit personal and geographical names throughout the book. He referred to introduced English place names only when he discussed circumstances and events concerning the colonial attitude of explorers and whalers. Boas did not like, and criticised strongly, their custom of disregarding aboriginal names in favour of making up their own place names (Boas 1885h:44). At that time this was the prevalent approach by colonial powers in many regions of the globe. He expressed his opinion clearly by writing: *"Indeed it can be deplored if indigenous names get lost because, like the Eskimo ones, they are so fitting; but then I have experienced considerable anger, annoyance and inconveniences by the numerous English names and the missing of indigenous names that I would have been prevented by this situation to make use of the explorer's right [to give names] anywhere. However, it is certainly more valuable scientifically to preserve the indigenous names than to write names of all meritorious or not so meritorious friends à la Ross and Hall on bays and foothills."* (Boas 1885h:51).

In the second chapter Boas dealt with the *History of Exploration* of the Northwest Passage in the North American Arctic as of the sixteenth century, concentrating on Baffin Land and particularly Cumberland Sound (Boas 1885h:23-39). He thoroughly quoted and reviewed the relevant literature, which was mainly by British explorers. He also touched upon the activities on the coast of Labrador of the missionaries of the protestant Moravian *Herrnhuter Brüdergemeinde*, the Herrnhut Unity of Brethren, and the first demographic assessment of Inuit in Cumberland Sound, made by one of their brethren in 1857-1858. Boas showed a particular interest in the expansion and impact of the whaling industry and provided an overview of American whaling activities in Cumberland Sound between 1846 and 1876 by listing ships' names and tonnage, home ports, whaling seasons, takes in oil, blubber, and baleen, as well as seals and walrus killed (Boas 1885h:32-33). He highlighted the fact that the aboriginal Inuit had become dependent on whalers with respect to employment, imported goods, foods, and guns for hunting. The rapid depletion of larger whales and other marine mammals led to a decline in commercial whaling, as Boas could observe himself during his stay at the Kekerten whaling station. He predicted the imminent demise of the industry, which would cause increased migration of Inuit to coasts where some whaling might still occur in the future (1885h:31).

In the third chapter entitled *Geography*, Boas presented an assessment of the physiogeography, geomorphology, and ice formations in southern Baffin Land within the areas he had surveyed personally with the help of Inuit and Wilhelm Weike (Boas 1885h:39-42 with six maps drawn by Inuit). This was all territory that had not been studied and surveyed before, thus Boas had to rely on Inuit knowledge, his own observations, and on comparisons drawn from his readings about other geographic regions. He provided precise and detailed descriptions and analyses of the geological and geomorphological landscapes, the lakes, rivers, and their drainage systems, the passes across ridges, and the traces of periglacial forms left by the last deglaciation. For these spatial analyses, particularly of the coastal outlines, he perused the maps drawn for him by Inuit, who showed a keen sense of scale (Spink & Moodie 1972:70-72, 90-93). Boas directly integrated the names, their origins and meanings that Inuit provided for locations, and spaces into his cartographic interpretations. By doing so, in fact, he fully acknowledged and recognized local Inuit environmental and geographical knowledge and concepts, putting them

on an equal level with western scientific paradigms and
practices. This was certainly a decisive step towards the full
acceptance of the oral tradition, literature, and history of
Inuit. He would express this more strongly later on when
engaged in the study of folklore (Boas 1904). He strength-
ened the validity of his sources on a personal level by identifying by name, location, and date each of the Inuit experts
who drew maps for him, thus recognizing their right to
individual intellectual property (1885h:43, 49).

Fig. 27. North side of Pangnirtung Fiord, Cumberland Sound,
about seven km east into the fiord, October 1883 (Sketch: *Franz Boas,
American Philosophical Society*)

Fig. 28. Nerselung Valley and Angiukak (Anngijuqqaaq) Mountain (1400 m) on the north side of Kingnait Fiord, Cumberland Sound, as seen from Karsak on the south side, October 1883 (Sketch: *Franz Boas*; *American Philosophical Society*)

In the last chapter, called *Anthropogeographie* Boas set out to explain and analyse "*... people's living conditions in their dependency upon the nature of the land*" by using approaches emerging in the fields of anthropogeography, ethnology, and sociology (Boas 1885h:62-90 with four maps drawn by Inuit). He warned that, due to the complexities involved in studying and obtaining data on human-environmental relations, the application of "*... hypotheses that are difficult to control might easily lead to false and deceptive theories*" and that "*the rendition of universally valid conclusions*" needs to be dealt with more cautiously than in the exact sciences by taking repetitive measurements (Boas 1885h:62). Using this premise and always relying on Inuit as his source, Boas discussed a range of issues: ecological framework, social organization and kinship relations, demographic structure and distribution,

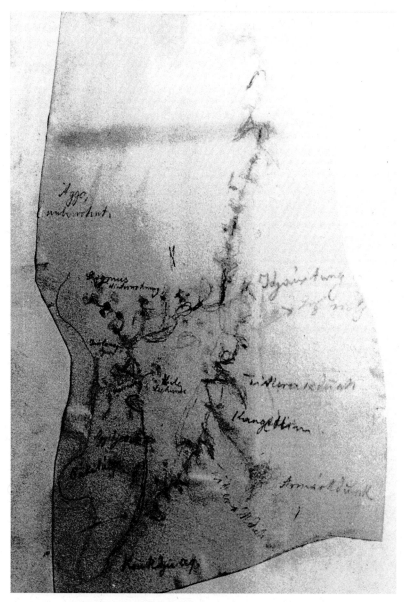

Fig. 29. Map of Lake Nettilling, Baffin Land, drawn by Mitik and Ocheitu (Oqaitung), January 1884 (*Ethnologisches Museum der Staatlichen Museen zu Berlin*; Photo: *Ludger Müller-Wille*, March 1983)

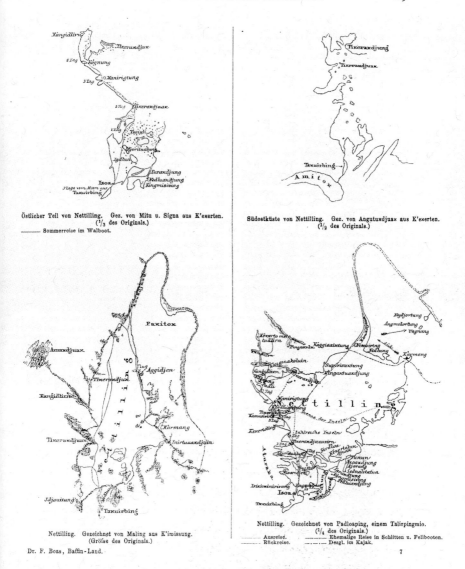

Östlicher Teil von Nettilling. Gez. von Mitu u. Signa aus K'exerten.
(¹/₃ des Originals.)
——— Sommerreise im Walboot.

Südostküste von Nettilling. Gez. von Angutuxdjuax aus K'exerten.
(¹/₂ des Originals.)

Nettilling. Gezeichnet von Maling aus K'imissung.
(Gröſse des Originals.)

Dr. F. Boas, Baffin-Land.

Nettilling. Gezeichnet von Padloaping, einem Talirpingmio.
(¹/₄ des Originals.)
············· Ausreise.   ——— Ehemalige Reise in Schlitten u. Fellbooten.
············· Rückreise.   —·—·— Desgl. im Kajak.

7

Fig. 30. Four maps of Lake Nettling, Baffin Land, drawn by Mitu and Signa, Angutuqdjuaq, Maling, and Padloaping, January 1884 (*Boas 1885h:49*)

settlement, migrations, and communication patterns, locations of resource utilization and seasonal economic cycles, and trade relations and other aspects of livelihood of Inuit in the Arctic environment. He also highlighted the rapidly growing dependency of Inuit on the already declining whaling industry. Boas concluded this section again with his earlier prediction that Inuit were a people threatened by *raschem Aussterben* or imminent extinction. He urged that further ethnographic studies should be undertaken to preserve elements of Inuit and other cultures in the explicit interest of the advancement and to the benefit of Western science (Boas 1885h:90). At that time and later, he did not seem to understand the internal dynamics and resilience of Inuit, and aboriginal cultures in general, that enabled them to adapt to future changes all the while maintaining their identity and cultural distinctness.

Following the last chapter, Appendix 1, entitled *Place Names*, lists all place names that Boas collected with Inuit with a section *Synonyma* that includes names given by explorers and whalers for some of the locations. In all, 930 Inuit place names are listed and shown on the various maps included in *Baffin-Land*, only a few non-Inuit names are indicated (Boas 1885h:90-93, Plate I with Inset Maps 1-6, Plate II; republished in black-and-white in revised form in 1888e:662-666, Plate II-III). These extraordinary and exceptional maps were the first representations of a comprehensive and intimate picture of the cultural landscape as seen by Inuit, the anthropogeography of Baffin Land (Müller-Wille & Weber Müller-Wille 2006; compare with work by Boas on Kwakiutl geographical names [Boas 1934b]). Boas single-handedly conducted the technical side of these systematic topographic surveys. In addition he took into account data on population distribution, settlement patterns, migratory movements, hunting practices and spatial extent of the use of resources. These maps allow a historical analysis of the changes in land use among the Inuit during the last one hundred and thirty years. Moreover the place names and related stories were the basis for Boas's understanding of human-environmental relations in the Arctic environment.

To gain access to the human dimension of the natural environment, Boas let individual Inuit or small groups explain the range of their geographical knowledge by identifying places and areas which they had given names in return for compensation in goods and food,. The maps drawn by Inuit are testimony to their keen perception and deep knowledge of their surroundings. The precision of Boas's cartographic and toponymic representations was proven by a survey that Linna Weber Müller-Wille, Christine Mason, our assistant and my former student, and I conducted with Inuit experts in Pangnirtung in July and August 1984. Some of the experts were descended from Inuit with whom Boas worked in 1883-1884. The survey covered the region of Cumberland Sound and eastward to Davis Strait. The oldest among the experts, eighty-four-year-old Aksayuk Etuangat, knew and confirmed most of the place names and their locations in Boas's published list and maps. We had brought copies to the surveys and displayed these materials in an Open House for the community of Pangnirtung. The Inuit were surprised to learn that their very own place names had existed in print in Germany for over one hundred years without them knowing about it (Müller-Wille & Weber Müller-Wille 2006).

Boas's *Baffin-Land* soon found attention in German geographical circles and was favourably reviewed in various

Fig. 31. Aksayuk Etuangat (right) and Allan Angmarlik recording place names in Pangnirtung, Cumberland Sound, Northwest Territories [Nunavut], August 1984 (Photo: *Ludger Müller-Wille*)

Fig. 32. Place name survey team at work in Pangnirtung; Aksayuk Etuangat (right), Allan Angmarlik, Linna Weber Müller-Wille, and Christine Mason, August 1984 (Photo: *Ludger Müller-Wille*)

Fig. 33. Display of Franz Boas's photos and map at an Open House in Pangnirtung, August 1984 (Photo: *Ludger Müller-Wille*)

scientific journals by highly respected colleagues such as Georg Gerland (Straßburg), Alfred Kirchhoff (Halle), Otto Krümmel (Kiel), and Hermann Wagner (Göttingen). Boas was encouraged by this reception and, on January 19, 1886, he filed his application, written in Latin, for the *Habilitation* procedure in *geographica physica*, physical geography, addressed to all professors of the Faculty of Philosophy at the *Friedrich-Wilhelms-Universität* in Berlin. He was accepted by the faculty and admitted to the *Habilitations-verfahren* to obtain the *venia legendi* (January 19, 1886, HUBA). Along with the application he submitted official documents, his dissertation, twelve publications (eight in German and four in English; eight dealt with Inuit and the Arctic, Boas 1883a-b, 1884a, 1885c-h), a list of three topics for the two compulsory lectures, and his curriculum vitae.

By the end of March 1886, the Dean of the Faculty of Philosophy, Wilhelm Scherer, received the reports by the two assigned assessors, Wilhelm von Bezold, meteorologist and Boas's academic mentor appointed by the faculty, and Heinrich Kiepert, historical geographer and second assessor. The assessment by von Bezold was very positive. He recommended approval stating that *"the spirit of serious and upright research emanates from all* [his works]*"* (March 15, 1886, HUBA). Kiepert voiced strong reservations, stating that Boas's publications were nothing more than travel reports *"... that we have received manifold from practical and unschooled seafarers."* He nonetheless gave his approval reluctantly with the condition that the list of lectures to be held by Boas be revised to show he was capable of dealing with general matters in geography, particularly physical geography (March 25, 1886, HUBA).

After some discussions Scherer asked Boas to lecture on two physical topics. On May 27, 1886 he spoke on *The Ice Conditions of the Arctic Ocean* before thirty-four faculty members, who all signed off and approved his *Habilitation*. The final step required of Boas was to give the public *Praelectio* on *Concerning the Cañon Area of the Colorado* on June 5 (handwritten lecture manuscripts in APS/FBPP, Boas 1885l-m). After that, just a month before he turned twenty-eight, he received the official certificate and obtained the title *Dr. habil.* and the *venia legendi* for geography as *Privatdozent* with the privilege to give courses in both geography and ethnography. Later in the fall of 1886, Boas mentioned to his parents in a letter from British Columbia where he had begun to conduct research (November 18, 1886, APS/FBFP; Zumwalt 2013b) that he had submitted a detailed teaching program with six courses (lectures, colloquia, and excursions)—a total of ten hours a week—which was included in the catalogue for the 1887 summer term at the *Friedrich-Wilhelms-Universität zu Berlin*. The courses were to cover separately the history of polar exploration, oceanography, geography of North America, ethnography of the Northwest Coast, and itinerary survey technique with excursions (HUBA, catalogue 1887). Boas never taught these courses. By late 1886, with the prospect of employment with the magazine *Science*, he had definitely decided to stay in the United States and cancelled all courses, thus relinquishing the position as a docent at the university in Berlin (letter to parents, December 31, 1886, APS/FBFP).

10

Getting settled in the United States, 1886-1888: Ethnological and Geographical Writings

Boas did not want to wait and seek an academic position in Germany, although he did take precautions to return if the need would arise. Only one month after his inaugural lecture on July 8, 1886, accompanied by his older sister Antonie, he left first for England. In London he met with Alfred Selwyn, head of the Geological Survey of Canada in Ottawa, to discuss his future research plans on the Northwest Coast in British Columbia in Canada. Earlier in 1886, together with James Mutch, Boas had explored plans to spend the winter 1886-1887, accompanied again by Wilhelm Weike, at the Kekerten whaling station to extend his research into Inuit tales and beliefs. For that purpose he had also contacted the geologist Robert Bell, responsible for Arctic research in the Geological Survey of Canada, to inquire about passage on a government research vessel from Halifax to Baffin Land that summer. Bell had obtained official approval and informed Boas that the ship would leave in late June. Boas declined the offer partly because of timing, but also because his research interests had shifted. Moreover it seemed he could not imagine being isolated again in Cumberland Sound and separated from Marie, his future wife, for a whole year. What's more, British Columbia was accessible by train through the United States or Canada making travelling and mobility easier and more convenient. Boas would never return to the Arctic to conduct research directly with Inuit in their homeland (Müller-Wille & Gieseking 2011:263).

On July 14, 1886 Antonie and he boarded the steamer *Eider* in Southampton and landed in New York City on July 27 where he applied to become an immigrant in the United States (Boas, N. 2004:75). He joined Marie and her family in New York City and by mid-September he left again. This time he was travelling by train to the Pacific Northwest through the United States and then to British Columbia to begin his long-term research and relationship with the aboriginal peoples of the Northwest Coast in Canada (Zumwalt 2013b). Adolf Bastian and other scholars had encouraged him to extend his research across the North American continent to connect his Arctic research with the West, in fact, looking at an ethnographic profile cutting through different geographical and ecological regions from East to West. He had secured very little funding for the first trip, but obtained more secure financing to expand his work out West in the years to follow. By December 1886 he was back in New York City from his first field research trip in Canada after his Arctic sojourn (Cole 1999:99-104).

In late January 1887, Boas managed to land his first paid job in the United States as an *"assistant editor with special attention to geography"* with the journal *Science*, in which he had already published in early 1885. On February 1, 1887, on *Science* letterhead, he wrote Felix von Luschan, assistant in ethnology at the Royal Museums in Berlin, to announce that he had *"now joined the journalists"* to start a new column on geography and ethnology in an aim to get Americans interested in such subjects and make the journal an essential source for Europeans wishing to learn about America (Dürr et al 1992:177). As it turned out, Boas became quite a proficient journalist, and rapidly integrated into the English-speaking world.

Now with a steady income secured, Franz Boas and Marie Krackowizer married in New York City on March 10, 1887. This was the beginning of Boas's American life. He stayed with *Science* until early 1889 and then moved into his first academic position at Clark University in Worcester, Massachusetts, where he taught from 1889 to 1892. He became a naturalized United States citizen on February 23, 1892 (APS/FBFP, Zumwalt 2013b). In late 1892 he took the position as an assistant curator in the Anthropological Section of the 1893 World's Columbian Exposition in Chicago. In 1894 he began work as a research assistant at the American Museum of Natural History in New York City, where he held a curatorship between 1896 and 1905. His career would finally take him to fill a secure position at Columbia University, first as lecturer in 1896 and then as professor of anthropology in 1899. He held a parallel teaching position at Barnard College from 1919 to 1928. In 1936 he retired from Columbia University and remained emeritus professor till his death on December 21, 1942 (for biographical details see Cole 1999, Boas, N. 2004, Zumwalt 2013a).

Once Boas had begun work as a professional writer his output of English language publications increased considerably, with some sixty items published on a broad variety of topics, mainly on geographical matters, in *Science* between 1885 and 1890 alone. In turn, the number of his German language articles decreased. In 1887 and 1888 Boas produced a large number of publications, seventy-eight in all, twenty-two of which dealt with Inuit, Baffin Land, and Arctic exploration. They included the much-awaited voluminous edition of *The Central Eskimo*. Six publications on those topics were still in German (Andrews and others 1943:69-72).

11

Inuit Tales and Lexicon, Arctic Ice and Climate, 1887-1894: Assessing Culture, Language, and Nature

Boas continued the study of the world of Inuit tales and beliefs, which he had begun earlier (Boas 1885f). He published a detailed article in German on *The Religious Beliefs and Some Customs of the Central Eskimos* (Boas 1887a) in which he discussed the distribution, reach, and relationship of particular Inuit tales and customs across Baffin Land and Greenland. He drew from the available literature by explorers and Moravian missionaries, but in particular from publications by Rink (Boas 1883c, 1887b, latter based on 1885f). He also compared some Inuit vocabularies from various regions and analysed specific tales.

Boas's last publication in German on Inuit oral traditions, *Tales of the Eskimo from Baffin Land* (Boas 1888c) in the *Verhandlungen der Berliner Gesellschaft für Anthropologie, Ethnologie und Urgeschichte*, was triggered by the puritanical censorship applied by the Smithsonian Institution to some tales, and specifically to *Ititaujang*, "The One

Like an Anus," that he had included in *The Central Eskimo.*
Boas felt obliged to explain this situation in a footnote:
*"This tradition was curtailed, as some parts were considered
inappropriate for publication."* (Boas 1888e:616). To protect
the authenticity and integrity of Inuit who related the tales
and his own transliteration, Boas submitted the complete
German translation to the Berlin Society to be read at its
meeting on October 20, 1887. He prefaced the submission
by writing: *"Because the editors of the report* [of the Bureau
of Ethnology] *eradicated, however, some obscene passages
that were not deemed appropriate to the character of the
annual report, I herewith render the respective tales in their
entirety."* (Boas 1888c:398). The Society accepted and
promptly published the complete text of the four tales.

Boas's interest in beliefs, tales, and songs of the Inuit
continued for some years despite his expanding research
with Kwakiutl in British Columbia. In 1889 Rink, who also
reviewed *The Central Eskimo* (Rink 1890), and Boas jointly
published an article in the newly founded *Journal of
American Folk-Lore* in which they presented the original
Inuktitut texts with English translation (Rink & Boas 1889).
The use of the assumed authentic, unaltered text, was certainly suggested by Rink, but also had to do with Boas
being co-founder of the American Folklore Society and its
journal in 1888. The journal's focus was on both literary
and anthropological documentation and interpretation of
oral literature and required original texts (Zumwalt 1988:13-
21). Some years earlier Boas had lauded Rink's seminal
work on Inuit languages in a review (Boas 1886b). In later
years, he presented more Inuit tales and songs, even adding
music scores in Inuktitut and/or in English translation
(1894b-c, 1897, 1904, 1922). Boas printed the original version

of the tales and songs exactly as he had jotted them down while repeatedly listening to Inuit on Baffin Land (Müller-Wille, ed. 1998:249-254). Over the years Boas broadened his research interests to work on several aboriginal languages in North America, which led to major initiatives and contributions to the emergence of linguistic anthropology as a separate field (Schott 1994).

In 1894, ten years after his return from the Arctic, Boas published his last item on Inuit in German, a lexicon or vocabulary with some 2,200 entries, entitled *The Eskimo Dialect of Cumberland Sound* (Boas 1894a). It included words, with some conjugations and derivations, phrases, 540 toponyms (Boas 1885h:90-95), and 275 personal names (Krupnik & Müller-Wille 2010:378-390). He translated all entries, as much as he could, into German. This list most likely comprised all that he had ever collected and learned in Inuktitut during his stay with the Inuit. He cross-checked his material with different sources, marked the items accordingly, and demonstrated a closer linguistic relationship between Inuit along the coast of Labrador and Baffin Land than with Greenland. In his short introduction Boas does not mention Rink directly or whether Rink had seen the list before he died. Since Boas had sent Rink all his linguistic materials already in 1885, it can be assumed that Boas integrated all of Rink's comments and suggestions. Boas also mentioned that this lexicon would be followed by another publication to include texts, comments on phonetics, grammar, and words (Boas 1894a:97). In 1887 Boas had already stated that he had "... *collected a vocabulary of perhaps a thousand words and some slight account of the grammar of the language*." (Pilling 1887:12) These intentions were never realized by Boas and would now require the reconstruction of Boas's complete original handwritten materials in Inuktitut that are held by the American Philosophical Society in Philadelphia and the Danish Royal Library in Copenhagen, and possibly in other places.

In a short illustrated publication *Das Fadenspiel*, The Cat's Cradle, Boas showed his keen interest in ethnographic details of Inuit culture concerning art and games, including those using strings. He commented on the fact that he had observed such games among the Inuit and found them to be authentic and widely spread among various populations throughout the North American Arctic (Boas 1888b, also 1888e:569-570). In an aim to obtain more Inuit oral traditions, customs, and ethnographic objects, Boas continued to maintain contact with American whaling captains through extensive correspondence, especially with James Mutch, with whom he exchanged letters until the early 1920s (Harper 2008). These whalers kept him informed about changes in the Canadian Arctic from Baffin Land to the western coast of Hudson Bay. They sent him extensive materials, mainly in English, which Boas collated, edited, and published in two major compendia, giving them full credit as collaborators (Boas 1901, 1907). These publications and *The Central Eskimo* continue to be some of the main reference sources for the history and anthropology of Inuit. Moreover, for Inuit they are a source for identifying with their own history and for enhancing and developing their language and culture. Boas would be delighted and astonished to learn about such developments among the modern Inuit. Had he not predicted the demise and extinction of Inuit culture within a few decades after his stay with them in the 1880s (Boas 1885b, 1888h:90)?

Der Eskimo-Dialekt des Cumberland-Sundes.

Von Franz Boas.

Das nachfolgende Material wurde auf einer Reise in Baffin-Land in den Jahren 1883 und 1884 gesammelt. Der Dialekt, auf welchen sich dasselbe bezieht, wird im Cumberland-Sunde und an den wenig nördlicher gelegenen Theilen des Westküste der Baffins-Bay gesprochen. Der Dialekt lehnt sich enger an den von Labrador als an den von Grönland an, was uns nicht Wunder nehmen darf, da die Sitten und Gebräuche der Stämme ebenfalls denen von Labrador ähnlicher sind, als denen von Grönland.

Ich habe lange mit der Veröffentlichung des von mir gesammelten Materiales gezögert, da dasselbe in vielen Beziehungen mangelhaft und unvollkommen ist. Es sind die Resultate einer Erstlingsreise und die mangelnde Erfahrung des Sammlers zeigt sich in den Lücken und Unvollkommenheiten des Materials. Ich war mir der Wichtigkeit sprachlicher Studien während der ganzen Reise nicht klar bewusst, da ich glaubte, die Studien der grönländischen und labradorischen Missionäre gäben ein genügendes Bild der Eskimosprache, und concentrirte meine Arbeit auf geographische und ethnologische Probleme. Es stellte sich erst nach meiner Rückkehr heraus, als ich versuchte, die mitgebrachten Texte übersetzen zu lassen, ein wie interessantes Studium die alterthümlichen Texte, die eigenthümliche Geheimsprache der Angakut und die dialektischen Abweichungen bieten. Nach reiflicher Ueberlegung scheint mir das gesammelte Material doch genug Neues zu bieten, um eine Veröffentlichung zu rechtfertigen.

Der vorliegende Aufsatz enthält das gesammelte Vocabular, verglichen mit dem Wortschatze von Labrador und Grönland. Ein folgender Aufsatz soll die Texte, Phonetik, Grammatik und eine Discussion des Vocabulars enthalten.

Ich habe das von den grönländischen Missionären aufgestellte Alphabet benützt, doch sind lange Vocale nur durch Längen (—) angedeutet und Accente der Worte mehrfach angegeben. Das velare k ist durch q ausgedrückt, das deutsche ch in Bach durch x. Alle anderen Buchstaben werden wie im Deutschen ausgesprochen.

Abkürzungen: L. = Labrador, G. = Grönland, E. = Eigenname, O. = Ortsname.

Mittheilungen d. Anthrop. Gesellsch. in Wien. Bd. XXIV. 1894.

A.

a pl. mit Suff. 3. Person, angin. Seitenspitze des Vogelspfeils. G. dq.

agia, pl. agidjen Geweihsprosse, pl. auch Ortsname.

aja Mutters Schwester L., G.

ainga, aikolua seines Bruders Frau. L. ai.

ailang Schweiss, auch E., L. ailak, G. ailaq.

aipa der andere mit Suff. 3. Person., L., G. aipuq; aipa — aipa der eine — der andere, aipunga der andere mit Suff.

aisicarpoq er geht auf Seehundsjagd im Winter. — siarpoq er geht aus nach —

Aise'ang E.

aisivang Spinne, auch E., L. asivak, G. ausiaq.

aisivoluaq danke (siehe G. aso genug!).

Aisoin E.

aiviq dual. aiving, pl. aivin Walross, L. aivek, G. auveq.

aivoq er geht zu holen, L. aivok, G. aica er holt es.

aqpe'it er trägt sie; ainiedlaranuk, ai — gehen zu holen —, dlarpoq sehr;

aitirtoq gehend nach —, aititietaminga wenn er selbst nicht geht und holt;

aivasima'meta wenn sie gegangen sind, etwas zu holen, — simavoq Perfect.

ajang Querholz des Kajak, L. ajak, G. ajuq.

ajeqpurpoq, er stützt sich auf die Hände, G. ajaperpoq; ajaqu'tirpoq es ist ein Regenbogen da;

aje'gang Bilboquet, ajautang Stock dazu: ajega'tang äusserer Rand der Augenhöhle;

aje'ksaung Gabel, Sikosuilaq-Dialekt, O. ajokitarpoq ein Spiel, aju'ktang Ball;

aju'ktaun Stock zum Ballschlagen, ajuktaq'tung das Ballschlagen, aja'rorpoq er spielt das Fadenspiel.

Aje'paung O.

a'jorang Spalt im Eise (Sprungspalt, nicht die Spalten am Ebbestrande), L. ajorak.

ojurnaqpoq es ist schwierig, ajurnianigmen da es nicht schwierig ist (G. — ngingmat).

ajorunga sein Brudersohn, L, G. ujoruk.

ajuarng, Dual. ajuung, pl. ajuan Beule, L. ajuak, G. ajuaq.

ugoq, pl. again Hand, L. agguk, G. agssuk;

a'gaun Unterarm und Handgelenk, auch O., uga'paung Fingerspitze, auch O. agi'qpit tunua Dein Handrücken.

agartsorutika mein Mittel zur Verwandlung (?).

agia Feile, L. aggiak, G. agiuq.

Agiara'dlo E.

agirpoq er nähert sich, L. aggerpok, G. aggerpoq.

agim Ente. L., ajjek, G. agdleq;

Agirtü'jung reich an Enten O.

ago Wetterseite, L. ago, G. agssoq.

agu er sagt ja (a ja, — goq, — goq sagt —).

A'gudlung E.

Fig. 34. Title page of Franz Boas's article *"The Eskimo Dialect of Cumberland Sound"* (*Boas 1894a*; reader's markings by author)

In 1886, reviewing the results of the Canadian *Neptune* expedition of 1884, Boas discussed emerging proposals to build a branch rail line from Winnipeg connecting the recently completed transcontinental railroad with York Factory on Hudson Bay (Boas 1886a). From there, shipping larger volumes of grain and other commodities in trade with Great Britain would be facilitated. The *Neptune* was sent out to survey ice conditions. In his review, Boas was not optimistic that the seasonal ice conditions would allow extended shipping. Technological advances in rail and maritime transport, however, proved him wrong. It took a few more decades of studies and ensuing investment before a rail link was constructed to Fort Churchill in 1929 to open shipping lanes between Hudson Bay and the Atlantic.

During his stay on Baffin Land Boas made extensive observations of changing ice conditions and formations and their influence on mobility and resource utilization by both Inuit and whalers (Boas 1885l). Residing now in New York City, he was close to the home bases of the American whaling industry on the coast of Connecticut. He seized this opportunity and collected further detailed data on the spatial extent and temporal fluctuations of sea-ice from logbooks kept by whalers (Boas 1888a). These data included information on fast ice, locations of polynya—open water surrounded by sea ice—and ice-free areas along the coastal areas of southeastern Baffin Land for a thirty-five-year period between 1852 and 1887. He summarized and extrapolated the data systematically, including his own observations from 1883-1884, and produced a map showing the yearly fluctuations in ice conditions (Boas 1888a). He remarked on the accuracy of data provided by the whalers and discussed the conditions during individual years. Boas felt that the reasons for annual fluctuations were related to changing currents, including tides, and the topography of the coastline, a plausible explanation based on the status of research at the time.

In another article, submitted to the prestigious *Annalen der Hydrologie und maritimen Meteorologie* in February 1888, Boas tabulated all meteorological measurements taken by Wilhelm Düwel (William Duval), James Mutch, Wilhelm Weike, and himself at two whaling stations, one on the eastern and the other on the western side of Cumberland Sound, in 1883-1884 (Boas 1888d). The data were to be complemented by the more extensive and regular recordings by the German polar research station in Kingua for the year 1882-1883, but those only appeared in publications in the early 1890s (Müller-Wille, ed. 1998:6-11). Although there were gaps in the readings, the measurements were quite exact for temperature, wind direction and force, barometric level, precipitation, and cloud cover. Analysing the results, Boas provided the first scientific attempt at a broader synopsis of regional climate conditions in the Arctic.

These historical meteorological data, provided in these two articles, are an important and extremely valuable source for the analysis of climatic change over the past one hundred thirty years. With these publications Boas showed his scientific skills, flexibility, and adaptability to move between physical sciences on the one side and social sciences on the other. He gave much thought to the scientific approaches and the dichotomy between exact sciences, which were aimed at the deduction of *"laws of nature,"* and that seemingly allowed explanations and predictions, and the investigation of the historical progression of human

social behaviour in relation to the physical environment.
Boas had pondered about those issues since he returned
from the Arctic in September 1884. Now in November 1887
he debated these matters in the article *The Study of
Geography* (Boas 1887-1888 - Sc 1, reprint Boas 1940a) at a
juncture when geography had not yet emerged as a full-
fledged academic discipline in the United States. That essay
can be seen as a threshold in Boas's scientific thoughts
dealing with methodological approaches, as he continued
to understand them within the realm of social sciences and
in particular in the emerging field of cultural anthropology.
Boas identified geography as a *"descriptive science,"* whose
*"... center of interest is the geographical phenomenon as a
whole,"* meaning both the natural environment and human
world. He also recognized the *"conflicting view of natural-
ists and historians in treating geographical subjects"* (Boas
1887-1888 - Sc 1). The discussion of these Boasian ideas has
not waned, as is expressed by the recent inclusion of that
article in major textbooks for geography and anthropology
(Agnew et al. 1996:173-180, Stocking 1996:9-16) and the continued attention and discussion in the literature (Stocking
1965, Speth 1978, Bunzl 1996:56-58, Liss 1996:155-156, Cole
1999:122, Lewis 2001, 2008).

Fig. 35. Iceberg at the entrance of Cumberland Sound, Baffin Land, July 28, 1883 (Sketch: *Franz Boas*; *American Philosophical Society*)

Fig. 36. Iceberg with a cave at the entrance of Cumberland Sound, Baffin Land, July 28, 1883 (Sketch: *Franz Boas*; *American Philosophical Society*)

Fig. 37. Drifting iceberg off Cumberland Sound, early August 1883
(Photo: *Franz Boas*; *American Philosophical Society*)

Fig. 38. Calving iceberg off Cumberland Sound, early August 1883
(Photo: *Franz Boas*; *American Philosophical Society*)

Lasting Contributions by Franz Boas: Knowledge, Science, and Universality of Equality

Since his youth as a pupil with a keen interest in natural history and later as a student of natural sciences, geography, and philosophy Boas showed determination, aptness, and curiosity in the pursuit of knowledge. These characteristics were complemented by a strong sense of duty and responsibility towards people and society blended with the background of German Jewish family that fostered liberal and cosmopolitan ideals. Boas's socialization was also broadened and enhanced by an international network of relatives and their social, economic, and political affiliations (Brilling 1966, Bender-Wittmann 2007). Fulfilling his personal and scientific ambitions and satisfying his vision for life were not easy matters. He understood that he had to excel in whatever he pursued to be recognized, particularly in academic surroundings. His first testing grounds were physics and psychophysics, which he abandoned to engage fully in geography in the broadest sense, combining natural and human aspects to study the human-environmental relations

under specific physical conditions. His expansion into ethnology and ethnography was a natural and logical step, once
he had begun research with the Inuit. His excellent accom-
plishments in these various scientific realms were explained
in the previous chapters in the review of all his German
language writings on Inuit and the Arctic environment.
Those publications, varying in length and numbering forty-
two items or about six percent of his total production of
publications, are a small but quite important part of his
bibliography. They have been, in my opinion, neglected to
a large degree with regard to the historical consideration of
Boas's contribution to the study of Inuit cultural history,
geography, and anthropology.

Those early German publications focussed thematically
on physical geography, anthropogeography with the cartographic representation of topography and toponymy, as
well as on oral history through tales, and the history of
exploration and whaling. This vast material, now dating
back more than one hundred thirty years, represents an
invaluable source of the cultural history of the Inuit in the
Canadian Arctic. Appreciation of these contributions by
English language readers will make them more accessible,
particularly to Inuit knowing also English today, who want
to understand and learn about the living conditions, culture, beliefs, and language of their forebears in the Arctic
in the late nineteenth century. That was the period of the
modern wave of external intrusions by explorers and
whalers and barely one to two decades before Christian
missionaries such as those of the Anglican Church began
their activities and caused major social and cultural
changes in Inuit society. The increased awareness of these
sources will allow a critical examination of the data col-

lected and presented by Boas and relate them in an appropriate way to the present and future of Inuit culture.

Today, Boas's influence on the field of Arctic anthropology is still felt through his publications and museum work on ethnographic collections. During his active academic life he also had an impact in education, where he introduced references to Inuit to compare cultures, and, to some degree, in his supervision of graduate students while professor of anthropology at Columbia University for some forty years. Boas was an extraordinary mentor to many students, encouraging women in particular to study and complete their degrees (Zumwalt 2012). Between 1901 and 1939 he supervised forty-seven graduate students, twenty-six men and twenty-one women, who took their doctorates with him and published their dissertations based on field research in many parts of the world. Hardly any of Boas's students followed his early steps to conduct research with the Inuit. In 1897-1898 Alfred Louis Kroeber, one of the first students Boas taught in anthropology, studied the life and customs of the six Inuit whom Robert E. Peary brought from Greenland to New York. They became wards of the American Museum of Natural History, where Boas was working at the time (for details on their life stories and fate see Harper 2000). Kroeber published a lengthy treatise, as it were, in the footsteps of Boas's *The Central Eskimo* (Kroeber 1899). Later, as Boas's first doctoral student in anthropology at Columbia University, he wrote a short twenty-eight-page dissertation on decorative art among the Arapaho (Kroeber 1901). One other student, Frederica de Laguna, conducted research in Greenland in the late 1920s, advised by Danish anthropologists, and took her doctoral degree with Boas in 1933. She pursued a life-long career in

Arctic anthropology (data on students in anthropology at Columbia University, Zumwalt 2013b).

Later on in his life, through scientific, political, and personal engagement, Boas devoted much attention as a social activist to the issues of race and culture as well as to racial relations and perceptions with regard to the universal equality of human beings. It can be argued that the formulation of that axiom had its origin in his encounters and experiences with the Inuit. On January 22, 1884, travelling with Inuit on the pack ice in Cumberland Sound, he wrote in his letter-diary to Marie in deep self-reflection of what would lie in store for him once he returned from the Arctic: *"And what I want, what I will live and die for, is equal rights for all, equal opportunities to* [work] *and strive for poor and rich! Don't you think that when one has done even a little toward this, this is more than the whole of science together?"* (Müller-Wille, ed. 1998:171). Almost five decades later, on July 30, 1931 in his last public speech in Germany at his Alma mater, *Christian-Albrechts-Universität zu Kiel*, Boas adamantly and convincingly asserted his position against *"racial distinction and racial antipathy"* and condemned racial discrimination and persecution outright (Boas 1932). The occasion was his golden doctoral anniversary and the awarding of an honorary doctoral degree in medicine. Boas argued that *"*[t]*he behaviour of a people is not intrinsically defined by biological lineage, but by cultural tradition"* (Boas 1932:19). On the eightieth anniversary of its publication Boas's speech was republished in Kiel (Boas 1932 [2012]). In the postscript to that reissue Friedrich Pöhl, philosopher and anthropologist, pointed to Boas's deep conviction *"that pseudo-scientific racism is a monstrous fallacy or a shameless lie."* (Pöhl 2012:397). Franz Boas fought for the universality of human rights and the equality of all individuals. He hoped in that way to advance the moral quality of societies and cultures.

Less than two years later after his momentous and powerful speech in Kiel, on March 27, 1933, just two months after Hitler's usurpation of power and government in Germany, Franz Boas went public with his position against Nazi ideology, demagoguery, suppression, and exclusion of people based on race, religion, and different views, particularly with respect to the Jews in Germany. He sent a forthright Open Letter to the President of the German *Reich*, Paul von Hindenburg (*Offener Brief*, reprinted in Sundergeld 1980:185-188) raising his concerns and outrage over Nazi policies. This letter was distributed quite widely in Germany using clandestine means. It was a climax in Boas's personal and political actions to protest and become active. He further sought change by offering moral and financial support to numerous friends, colleagues, as well as close family members to flee Nazi Germany in time before the Nazis turned to the atrocities of liquidating people and committing genocide (Boas, N. 2004:232-261, Langenkämper 2009).

In February 1885 Boas published a quite revealing and honest paragraph in the second part of his newspaper series *Below the Arctic Circle* (Boas 1885b). He had explained to his readers how he had lived and conducted research with the Inuit in the Arctic. He closed with reflections on his intellectual development and emotional turmoil with respect to living with foreign people whom he now considered *"his Friends."* In the late 1800s, labels were used which would now be considered pejorative, but were not necessarily so at that time. Boas called the Inuit *Wilde* or

Savages and still used the term *Primitive People* almost sixty years after his stay on Baffin Land (Boas 1940b; Zumwalt 2013b).

Boas's intellectual shift evolved as he adopted ideas of those philosophers and scientists whose premises became a source of intellectual and mental strength. These were Immanuel Kant, Johann Gottfried Herder, Wilhelm von Humboldt, and Alexander von Humboldt, all of whom he learned to admire early on in his studies (for example on Herder see Broce 1986). With Kant, they all adhered to the axiom of the universality of humankind and expounded the essential importance of *"the diversity of languages and cultures and their world-views"* (Pöhl 2013). Boas's dedication to these ideals is shown in his reverence of Kant, whose works he took along to the Arctic, reading him intently for edification in his heartbreaking solitude on the ice off Anarnitung in Cumberland Sound on December 16, 1883 (Müller-Wille, ed. 1998:154).

It is fitting to end this essay with Boas's own words. They illustrate how his philosophical position changed from dividing humankind into *Kulturvölker* or civilized people and *Naturvölker* or primitive people to the encompassing universality and equality of all human beings, their cultures, and languages.

"Moreover I learned about the mores and customs of the natives, when we took trips by sled together and we were dependent upon each other for days on end, having to hunt together and share hunger and good times with one another. One need only keep company with the Eskimos in such a way for some weeks to recognize that they are not merely 'Wilde' or 'Savages'. To get to know character and mores closer, to gain comprehension of the many peculiar customs, requires

a long period of time of undeterred work and most careful attention with regard to every expression of Volksleben, a people's way of life, even if seemingly unimportant. Every new observation provides new subjects for thoughts and weaves a thread between other single observations until the whole shall merge into a fair image some day, in which we recognize under the strangest forms of living always again the thinking and feeling human being, who is closer to us in character than we could anticipate after a fleeting impression."

(Boas 1885b, Part II, February 22, 1885)

Acknowledgements

This book began with a brief paper entitled "Inuit and Arctic Environment: The Beginnings of Franz Boas's Scientific Approaches and Interpretations in the 1880s." I submitted the paper to the session "From Boas to Burch: One Hundred Years of Inuit Studies, 1880-1980" organized and chaired by Igor Krupnik at the Eighteenth Inuit Studies Conference, Smithsonian Institution, Washington, DC, United States, on October 25, 2012. I was not able to attend the meeting. In his collegial and friendly way, Igor Krupnik kindly agreed to read my presentation.

Rüdiger Schott, professor of ethnology and my doctoral supervisor at the *Westfälische Wilhelms-Universität* in Münster, introduced his first students to Franz Boas and his importance for ethnology in his first lecture course in the winter term of 1965-1966. This was the beginning of my reading of Boas's writings. Shortly after, in April 1966, it was the article by Bernhard Brilling (1966) that got me interested in Boas's personal and professional life. Since 1973 I have conducted research with Inuit in the Canadian Central Arctic and Cumberland Sound on Baffin Island in Nunavut and in Nunavik in Arctic Québec. These studies have led me to delve even deeper into Boas's scientific contributions, which enticed me, with Linna Weber Müller-

Wille, to carry out extensive place name surveys with the Inuit in Nunavik and Nunavut, and to transcribe and edit his Arctic journals and letters.

During a sabbatical year at the *Philipps-Universiät* in Marburg in 1982-1983 I began archival and literary research on Boas, visiting and contacting archives and libraries in Germany (Federal Republic of Germany and German Democratic Republic) and Denmark. During that stay, I also began to study Boas's toponymic and cartographic work on Baffin Island transferring Inuit place names from his original maps to modern topographic maps with the professional assistance of my wife Linna Weber Müller-Wille and the steadfast help of our children Ragnar, Verena, and Gwen Müller-Wille. In August 1984 my wife and I continued this project by working with Inuit on their toponyms around Cumberland Sound and along Davis Strait. In August 1983 I spent one week in the Manuscript Library of the American Philosophical Society in Philadelphia, Pennsylvania (USA) to study the Franz Boas Papers in the original and later on microfilms and paper copies. In succession, the manuscript librarians Stephen Catlett, Beth Carroll-Horrocks, and Charles B. Greifenstein have been very helpful to provide me with information and access to the archival sources over the years since 1983.

I am thankful for the amicable cooperation and kind support that I have received from colleagues over the years: Ursula Bender-Wittmann (Minden), Bernd Gieseking (Dortmund), Michi Knecht (Bremen), and Jürgen Langenkämper (Minden) in Germany, and Norman F. Boas (Mystic, CT) and Gertrude Michelson (Sandfield, MA), Franz Boas's grandchildren, in the United States. As so often before, Ragnar Müller-Wille (Saint-Lambert, Québec,

Canada) provided editorial comments and technical support preparing digital versions of the illustrations; his contribution is very much appreciated.

While preparing this manuscript, to my pleasant surprise, Rosemary Lévy Zumwalt initiated contact with me by sending a very kind note on January 1, 2013; she had read Franz Boas's Arctic diaries for her own research and complimented my editing and annotations. Since then she has inspired me with extensive correspondence and during phone calls enthusiastically discussing matters related to Franz Boas. I appreciate her interest, encouragement, and generosity freely sharing archival information with me.

Yvon Csonka (Neuchâtel, Switzerland), Igor Krupnik (Washington, DC, USA), Staffan Müller-Wille (Exeter, England), Pertti J. Pelto (Pune, India), Friedrich Pöhl (Innsbruck, Austria), William A. Weber (Boulder, Colorado, USA), and Rosemary Lévy Zumwalt (Dahlonega, Georgia, USA) kindly read drafts of the manuscript at various stages and made valuable comments and suggestions, most of which I could integrate. I am very grateful for their support, encouragement, and collegiality.

I would like to thank Robin Philpot of *Baraka Books* (Montréal, Québec, Canada), who, after having already published Wilhelm Weike's Arctic diaries by Bernd Gieseking and me in 2011, accepted to publish this book. He has been an encouraging and enthusiastic supporter by raising pertinent questions and problems and offering constructive editorial advice. As an author it has been my pleasure working with him again. A special thank-you goes to Josée Lalancette, *Folio Infographie* of Montréal, for her congenial approach to designing this book.

Linna Weber Müller-Wille (Saint-Lambert, Québec, Canada) reviewed and edited the manuscript, corrected and adjusted language and style in her gentle, patient, steady, and professional manner. I am ever grateful for her company and commitment. However, in the end, the content of this book is my responsibility.

List of People

(Sources are general encyclopaedias and the internet; FB - Franz Boas)

Abbes, Heinrich, 1856-1937, natural scientist; member of the German Polar Research station at Kingua in Cumberland Sound during the International Polar Year 1882-1883; studied in Hannover, Göttingen, and Heidelberg (doctorate 1894); lived and died in Braunschweig.

Ambronn, Leopold, 1854-1930, astronomer, deputy leader of the German Polar Research Station (see Abbes), professor of astronomy, *Georg-August-Universität* Göttingen.

Angmarlik, Allan, 1957-2000, educator, historian, Pangnirtung, Nunavut; on June 29, 2000, the artist Simata (Sam) Pitsiulak, owner and pilot of an ultra-light plane, took Angmarlik as a passenger on a flight from Kimmirut to Iqaluit, Nunavut. They crashed in inclement weather and both were tragically killed.

Bastian, Adolf, 1826-1905, ethnologist, founder and first director of the Museum of Ethnology in Berlin; ardent supporter of FB's scientific plans.

Bell, Robert, 1841-1917, geologist, physician, Arctic researcher, Geological Survey of Canada, Ottawa.

Bezold, Wilhelm von, 1837-1907, meteorologist, professor, *Friedrich-Wilhelms-Universität* Berlin.

Bessels, Emil, 1846-1888, physician, naturalist, explorer, European Arctic Ocean (1869-1870), scientist, *Polaris* Expedition (1871-1873) led by Charles Francis Hall, Smithsonian Institution, Washington.

Bismarck, Otto Fürst von, 1815-1898, *Reichskanzler* of the German *Reich*, 1871-1890.

Broce, Gerald L., 1942-2011, anthropologist; graduate student, *Westfälische Wilhelms-Universität* Münster (1966-68); professor, University of Colorado at Colorado Springs, Colorado.

Boas Family

(Franz Boas's parents)

Boas, Meier (also Meyer), 1823-1899, FB's father, retail merchant in Minden until 1887, moved to Berlin, fine goods exporter.

Boas, Sophie, 1828-1916, née Meyer, FB's mother, founder of a Fröbel Kindergarten and social activist in Minden until 1887, moved to Berlin.

(Franz Boas and his siblings by year of birth)

Boas, Helene, 1852-1857, Minden.

Boas, Antonie (Toni), 1855-1935, pianist, music teacher; married Ludwig Wohlauer, teacher, Berlin.

Boas, Franz, 1858-1942, physicist, geographer; first professor of anthropology, Columbia University, New York City, 1899-1936; engaged secretly to Marie Krackowizer, May 1883, married her in March 1887 (see Krackowizer).

Boas, Ernst, 1861, died less than one year old, Minden.

Boas, Hedwig (Hete), 1863-1949, married Rudolph Lehmann, teacher, Berlin; moved to the United States in 1939.

Boas, Aenna (Anna), 1867-1946, married Julius Urbach, brewer, Berlin; moved to Brasil in the 1930s.

Cole, Douglas, 1938-1997, historian, professor, Simon Fraser University, Vancouver, BC, Canada; biographer of Franz Boas.

Darwin, Charles, 1809-1882, British naturalist, evolutionist.

de Laguna, Frederica, 1906-2004, anthropologist, PhD with FB at Columbia University 1933, professor, Bryn Mawr College, Bryn Mawr, Pennsylvania.

Du Bois, W. E. B., 1868-1963), sociologist, historian, civil rights activist, professor, Atlanta University, Atlanta, Georgia; co-founder of National Association for the Advancement of Colored People (NAACP) in 1909.

Düwel, Wilhelm (William Duval), 1858-1931, German-American whaler and trader in Cumberland Sound, moved to the Arctic in

1879 and married an Inuit woman; his descendants live in Pangnirtung and other places.

Erdmann, Benno, 1851-1921, philosopher, professor, *Christian-Albrechts-Universität* Kiel, renowned Kantian scholar of his time; FB's professor in Kiel.

Etuangat, Aksayuk, 1901-1996, hunter, whaler, guide and assistant to government physicians, Pangnirtung, Nunavut; respected keeper of Inuit knowledge; his grandparents and parents met Franz Boas and Wilhelm Weike in 1883-1884.

Fischer, Theobald, 1846-1910, geographer, professor, *Rheinische Friedrich-Wilhems-Universität* Bonn, *Christian-Albrechts-Universität* Kiel, and *Philipps-Universität* Marburg; FB's professor in Bonn and Kiel.

Franklin, Sir John, 1786-1847, British Royal Navy officer, Arctic explorer who died as leader of the lost Northwest Passage Expedition in the summer of 1847.

Gerland, Georg, 1833-1919, geographer, geophysicist, ethnologist, professor, *Kaiser-Wilhelm-Universität* Straßburg, Elsaß/Alsace which was part of Germany from 1871 to 1918.

Greely, Adolphus, 1844-1935, US Army officer, leader of the Lady Franklin Bay Expedition 1881-1884, Ellesmere Island in Arctic Canada, part of the International Polar Year 1882-1883.

Haeckel, Ernst, 1834-1819, zoologist, philosopher, professor, *Universität* Jena; proponent of ecology.

Hall, Charles Francis, 1821-1871, Arctic explorer; leader of various American expeditions, died in 1871 during the *Polaris* Expedition 1871-1873.

Helmholtz, Hermann von, 1821-1894, physiologist, physicist, professor, *Friedrich-Wilhelms-Universität* Berlin; FB's supporter.

Herder, Johann Gottfried, 1744-1803, philosopher, philologist; studied oral literature and cultural identity.

Hindenburg, Paul von, 1847-1934, Prussian-German officer, chief of General Staff and General Field Marshal during WWI, second President of the German Reich during the Weimar Republic 1925-1933 and the Third Reich 1933-1934.

Hodges, Nathaniel Dana Carlisle, 1851-1927, editor, *Science* magazine, New York, 1885-1894.

Humboldt, Alexander von, 1769-1859, younger brother to Wilhelm von Humboldt, geographer, naturalist, travelled in Latin and North America 1799-1804 and Russia 1829; independent scholar, lived in Paris and Berlin.

Humboldt, Wilhelm von, 1767-1835, scholar, linguist, statesman, cofounder of the *Friedrich-Wilhelms-Universität* Berlin (after 1949: *Humboldt-Universität*) Berlin; reformer of the Prussian educational system.

Jacobi, Abraham, 1830-1919, widower of FB's mother's younger sister Fanny Meyer, 1833-1851; participant, Revolution of 1848 in Germany; pediatrician, City University of New York; life-time mentor and sponsor of FB.

Kant, Immanuel, 1724-1804, philosopher, professor, *Albertus-Universität* Königsberg, Prussia (today: Kaliningrad, Russian Federation).

Karsten, Gustav, 1820-1900, physicist, professor, *Christian-Albrechts-Universität* Kiel; FB's professor and supervisor in physics.

Kiepert, Heinrich, 1818-1899, historical geographer, cartographer, professor, *Friedrich-Wilhelms-Universität* Berlin; FB's *Habilitation* examiner in 1886.

Kirchhoff, Alfred, 1838-1907, geographer, professor, *Universität* Halle/Saale.

Kleinschmidt, Samuel, 1814-1886, Danish-German Moravian missionary, linguist and promoter of the Greenlandic language.

Klutschak, Heinrich W., 1848-1890, engineer, Prague; artist, Arctic and Antarctic traveller, member of the Franklin Search Expedition led by Frederick Schwatka in 1878-1880.

Krackowizer, Marie, 1861-1929, Austrian parents (father Ernst, 1821-1875, physician, New York City; participant, Revolution of 1848 in Vienna); married FB in 1887.

Kroeber, Alfred Louis, 1876-1960, anthropologist, FB's first doctoral student at Columbia University, professor of anthropology, University of California, Berkeley.

Krümmel, Otto, 1854-1912, geographer, oceanographer, professor, *Christian-Albrechts-Universität* Kiel.

Ladenburg, Albert, 1842-1911, chemist, professor and dean, *Christian-Albrechts-Universität* Kiel.

Levysohn, Arthur, 1841-1908, editor-in-chief, *Berliner Tageblatt*, Berlin.

Lindeman, Moritz,1823-1908, polar geographer, Bremen.

Luschan, Felix Ritter von, 1854-1924, physician, physical anthropologist, ethnographer, *Königliches Museum für Völkerkunde* (today: *Ethnologisches Museum*); professor, *Friedrich-Wilhelms-Universität* Berlin.

Mason, Otis Tufton, 1838-1908, ethnologist, curator, Smithsonian Institution, Washington.

Melville, George W., 1841-1912, Rear Admiral, US Navy, polar explorer, member of the *Jeannette* Expedition, 1879-1881.

Mosse, Rudolf, 1843-1920, owner, *Berliner Tageblatt*, Berlin.

Murdoch, John, 1852-1925, naturalist, ethnographer, member, International Polar Year Expedition in Alaska, 1881-1883; librarian, Smithsonian Institution, Washington.

Mutch, James (Jim), 1847-1931, whaler and trader, 1865-1922; manager of the Scottish whaling station at Kekerten, Baffin Land, 1883-1884; FB's translator - Inuktitut to English - and collaborator.

Neumayer, Georg von, 1826-1909, geophysicist, polar scientist, founder and head of the *Deutsche Seewarte* in Hamburg; prominent co-organizer of the International Polar Year 1882-1883.

Oqaitung, life dates unknown, Cumberland Sound, Baffin Land, employed by the German Polar Research Station at Kingua (1882-1883), hired by FB as helper in 1883-1884.

Parry, William Edward, 1790-1855, officer, British Navy, explorer in search of the Northwest Passage, led several expeditions between 1818-1827.

Peary, Robert E., 1856-1920, US Navy engineer, Arctic explorer (1886-1909) along coasts of Canada and Greenland, conducted his controversial drive to the North Pole in 1909.

Powell, John Wesley, 1834-1902, geologist, explorer, director, Bureau of Ethnology, Smithsonian Institution, Washington.

Ratzel, Friedrich, 1844-1904, travel journalist, zoologist, geographer, professor, *Universität* Leipzig; initiator of anthropogeography and political geography; strong supporter of FB's research plans in the Arctic.

Richthofen, Ferdinand Freiherr von, 1833-1905, geographer, professor, *Rheinische Friedrich-Wilhelms-Universität* Bonn, *Friedrich-Wilhelms-Universität* Berlin.

Rink, Hinrich Johannes, 1819-1893, naturalist, ethnographer, and administrator, Copenhagen; director of the Danish Royal Greenland Trading Department (*Den Kongelige Grønlandske Handel*).

Rittig, John, 1829-1885, journalist, editor, *New Yorker Staats-Zeitung*, New York; participant, Revolution of 1848 in Germany.

Scherer, Wilhelm, 1841-1886, philologist, Germanist, Vienna; professor, dean, *Friedrich-Wilhelms-Universität* Berlin.

Schott, Rüdiger, 1927-2012, ethnologist, Africanist, professor, *Westfälische Wilhelms-Universität* Münster.

Schurz, Carl, 1829-1906, participant, Revolution of 1848; American statesman, Civil War general, Secretary of the Interior, 1877-1881; FB's strong supporter.

Selwyn, Alfred, 1824-1902, geologist, director, Geological Survey of Canada, Ottawa.

Signa (Jimmy), 1848-1895, hunter, Cumberland Sound, employed by FB as helper (1883-1884).

Supan, Alexander, 1847-1920, geographer, cartographer, Vienna; editor, *Petermanns Geographische Mitteilungen*, Perthes Publisher, Gotha.

Tungilik, Marius Putjuut, 1957-2012, public servant, negotiator, journalist with CBC North, Naujaat/Repulse Bay, Nunavut; in 1988, first to state publicly sexual abuse of aboriginal children in residential schools in Canada which led to the Truth and Reconciliation Commission in Canada, 2007.

Tungilik, Mark, 1913-1986, hunter, carver, Naujaat/Repulse Bay; known for minute sculptures in soapstone, ivory, antler, and bone; father of Marius P. Tungilik.

Turner, Lucien, 1848-1909, US Army Signal Corps, naturalist, ethnographer, expeditions in Alaska (1874-1881) and Canada (1882-1884).

Virchow, Rudolf von, 1821-1902, physician, professor, *Friedrich-Wilhelms-Universität* and *Charité* Hospital; long-term member of the *Reichstag*, Berlin.

Wagner, Hermann, 1840-1929, geographer, professor, *Georg-August-Universität* Göttingen.

Weike, Wilhelm, 1859-1917, servant, Boas family (1879-1885), Minden; FB's servant on Baffin Land (1883-1884); moved to Berlin in early 1886 where he continued to work for the Boas family intermittently.

Wilhelm I., 1797-1888, King of Prussia, *Kaiser* of the German Reich (1871-1888).

Bibliography

Archival Sources

AEM - Archiv des Ethnologischen Museums der Staatlichen Museen zu Berlin (Preußischer Kulturbesitz), formerly Museum für Völkerkunde, Berlin, Germany. Inventory: America, Franz Boas Collection, IV A, Volume 2, 1862-1908 (accessed and reviewed in Berlin, March 1, 1983).

APS - American Philosophical Society, Philadelphia, Pennsylvania, USA. Franz Boas Collections (FBC), 1862-1942, B:B61. Franz Boas Professional Papers (FBPP), B:B61p; Franz Boas Family Papers (FBFP), Franz Boas Print Collection, B:B61p, B:B61.5 (accessed on site, August 15 to 19, 1983, and on copies and microfilms later on).

HUBA - Humboldt-Universität zu Berlin-Archiv, Berlin, Germany. Inventory: Philosophische Fakultät, Nr. 1213: Habilitationsakte Franz Boas, 19. Januar – 5. Juni 1886 (Faculty of Philosophy, No. 1213: *Habilitation* File Franz Boas, January 19 to June 5, 1886); course catalogue 1886-1887 (copy courtesy of Michi Knecht, May 23, 2008).

RLC - Royal Library, Copenhagen, Denmark. Rink Papers, *Eskimoiske Sagn og Sange samlede af Dr. F. Boas paa Baffins-Land* (Eskimo tales and songs collected by Dr. F. Boas on Baffin's Land). *Ny kongelige Samling* (New Royal Collection), No. 2488, IX, 50 pages, letters. Archive of The Royal Library, Copenhagen (accessed on site and materials copied, March 24, 1983)

Publications by Franz Boas

Note: Each item listed here has been checked and verified by the author for its bibliographical information. Annotations in italics and English translation of German titles in parenthesis were written by the author. Entries marked with an asterisk were found and identified by the author while conducting research on Franz Boas; they are not listed in the two available bibliographies of Franz Boas's published works (Andrews 1906, Andrews and others 1943).

Early in his career Boas kept hand-written lists of his publications for the *Habilitation* application and for his private use. The first chronological and almost complete bibliography was collated by Miss H. A. Andrews from Boston, whom Boas had got to know as an employee when they worked together at the magazine *Science* in 1887-1889. Not too much is known about Andrews, even her initials were never spelled out in print. Boas's correspondence tells us that Andrews socialized with the Boas family. Later on, he hired her as his trusted secretary at the American Museum of Natural History (AMNH) in 1897, where, among other matters, she looked after the publications of the *Jesup North Pacific Expedition* and became an indispensable professional support to Boas as stenographer, typist, editor, and office manager. When Boas left the AMNH in May 1905, he arranged that Andrews would join him at Columbia University (Cole 1999:221, 241-242, 247). She continued her work as an editor of manuscripts for publications until at least 1923, when she became very ill (Andrews to Boas, July 26, 1923, APS/FBPP, Boas, N. 2004:163, Zumwalt 2013b).

The bibliography compiled by H. A. Andrews listed 302 publications by Boas for the period of 1880-1906 (Andrews 1906:515-545) numbered consecutively (p 515-537), a list of editorships with 35 items (p 538-540), and a subject index (p 540-45). This bibliography was the last section in the *Festschrift*, called *Boas Anniversary Volume* (Laufer 1906), published at the occasion of the twenty-fifth anniversary of Franz Boas's doctorate at the *Christian-Albrechts-Universität zu Kiel* on August 9, 1881. Andrews succeeded in a Herculean bibliographic task and laid the groundwork for her successors, Boas's secretaries and diligent bibliographers, whose names are not all known and who, except for Andrews and Bertha C. Edel, never appeared in print.

These women continued the high standards set by Andrews of recording any future publication by Boas, who was a prolific author and writer. To recognize this great bibliographic achievement, on which many scholars have relied in their research on Boas, the known secretaries, all women, are listed here with as much information as could be ascertained. Albeit unusual, I would like to honour their commitment, diligence, and dedication, which, in the end, culminated in the second and ultimate bibliography of Boas's works, an indispensable tool and resource. It was published in 1943 under "H. A. Andrews and others 1943" as authors, and Bertha C. Edel, one of the secretaries, as editor. It listed 711 items numbered per year for 1880-1943, also cross-referencing and identifying reprints, translations, various editions, unpublished manuscripts, and editorships (p 67-109), and concluded with a detailed subject index (p 110-119).

Miss H. A. Andrews, secretary, editor 1897-1923.

Mildred Downs, secretary 1916-1919.

Esther Schiff Goldfrank (1896-1997), BA Barnard College 1918, secretary 1919-1922, anthropologist, worked with Elsie Clews Parsons and Ruth Benedict.

Ruth Leah Bernheim Bunzel (1898-1990), BA Barnard 1918, secretary 1922-1924, PhD with Boas, Columbia University 1929, anthropologist, lecturer and adjunct professor, Columbia University.

Bertha Cohen, secretary in 1931.

Ruth Bryan, secretary in the 1930s.

Bertha C. Edel (Mrs. Leon) (1904-1994), secretary in the mid-1930s, editor of the bibliography published in 1943.

(I am obliged to Rosemary Lévy Zumwalt for the personal information on the women mentioned; Zumwalt 2013b).

Boas, Franz

1880   Über die in der Jetztzeit stattfindenden Veränderungen der Oberflächenform der Erde (Concerning the changes in the earth's surface formation occurring at the present time). *New-Yorker Belletristisches Journal*, Friday, November 12, 1880.

1881   *Beiträge zur Erkenntnis der Farbe des Wassers* (Contributions to the Perception of the Colour of Water). Dr. phil., dissertation, Faculty of Philosophy, *Christian-Albrechts-Universität* at Kiel. Kiel: Schmidt & Klaunig. 44 pp., 4 tables, 2 figs.

1882-1884   Hand-written letters and journals in German, Germany
             - Baffin Land - New York, May 14, 1882 – September 20,
             1884 (APS/FBFP).
             *Published in German in Müller-Wille, ed. 1994:25-264 and
             in English in Müller-Wille, ed. 1998:33-266; see also an ear--
             lier English version in Cole 1983.*

1883a   Über die ehemalige Verbreitung der Eskimos im arktisch-
             amerikanischen Archipel (Concerning the earlier distribu-
             tion of the Eskimos in the Arctic American Archipelago).
             Zeitschrift der Gesellschaft für Erdkunde zu Berlin 18,2:118-
             136, Plate II.

1883b   Über die Wohnsitze der Neitchillik-Eskimos (Concerning
             the settlements of the Neitchillik-Eskimos). *Zeitschrift der
             Gesellschaft für Erdkunde zu Berlin* 18,3:222-233, Plate III.

1883c   B. [Boas, Franz]. Neueste Nachrichten über die Eskimos
             des Cumberland-Sund (Most recent news about the
             Eskimos of Cumberland Sound). *Deutsche Geographische
             Blätter* 6,2:172-178.
             *Assessment of Ludwig Kumlien's (1853-1902) "Ethnology.
             Fragmentary Notes on the Eskimo in Cumberland Sound"
             (Kumlien 1879:11-46).*

1883d*   Brief des Dr. Boas an den Vorstand der Gesellschaft für
             Erdkunde in Berlin. Kikkerton, 25. September 1883 (Letter
             by Dr. Boas to the Board of the Gesellschaft für Erdkunde
             in Berlin, Kikkerton, 25 September 1883). *Verhandlungen
             der Gesellschaft für Erdkunde zu Berlin* 10,9-10:476-477.

1883-1885   Articles in the *Berliner Tageblatt* (*BT* 1-18)
             See Müller-Wille 1984:119-120; English translations of *BT*
             3-18 in Boas 2009:1-53.

Trial articles

BT 1   F. B. [Franz Boas]. Der dritte deutsche Geographentag - I.
             Spezial-Bericht. Frankfurt a. M., 29. März [1883] (Third
             German Assembly of Geographers - I. Special Report.
             Frankfurt a. M., 29 March [1883]). *Berliner Tageblatt*,
             Evening Edition, Friday, 30 March 1883, Vol. 12,
             No. 148:2-3.

The annual assembly was held March 29-31, 1883. There was no article published by Boas on March 29, 1883 as listed in the bibliographies by H. A. Andrews (1906) and H. A. Andrews and others 1943).

BT 2   F. B. [Franz Boas]. Der dritte deutsche Geographentag - II. Spezial-Bericht. Frankfurt a. M., 30. März [1883] (Third German Assembly of Geographers - II. Special Report. Frankfurt a. M., 30 March [1883]). *Berliner Tageblatt*, Morning Edition, First Supplement, Sunday, 1 April 1883, Vol. 12, No. 151:4.

BT 3   [Franz Boas] Die Entdeckung der Nord-West-Durchfahrt. Original-Feuilleton des Berliner Tageblattes. (The discovery of the Northwest Passage. Original feature article of the Berliner Tageblatt). *Berliner Tageblatt*, Evening Edition (title page), Wednesday, 30 May 1883, Vol. 12, No. 241:1-2.

This article is signed "Editor of the Berliner Tageblatt", but was written by Boas, who included it in his personal and handwritten list of publications (APS/FBFP; also in Andrews 1906, Andrews and others 1943).

Commissioned articles

Articles BT 4 sent from Scotland and BT 6-8 from Cumberland Sound.

BT 4   Dr. F. Boas. Ins Eismeer! Reise-Vorbereitungen. Fahrt der "Germania" durch die Nordsee (Towards the Polar Sea! Travel preparations. Voyage by the "Germania" through the North Sea). *Berliner Tageblatt*, Morning Edition (title page), Saturday, 4 August 1883, Vol. 12, No. 359:1-2.

First report sent from Pentland Firth via fishing boat to Stroma, Scotland, and from there to Berlin on June 27, 1883.

BT 5   Dr. Fr. Boas. Die Polarexpedition von Charles Francis Hall (Charles Francis Hall's polar expedition). *Berliner Tageblatt*, Evening Edition (title page), Tuesday, 4 September 1883, Vol. 12, No. 417:1-2.

Article most likely written before departure in preparation for the series in the BT.

BT 6   Dr. F. Boas. Aus den Eis-Regionen. An Bord der Germania,
26. August 1883. Fahrt der Germania von Pentland Firth
nach Cumberland Sund (From the Frozen Lands. On
board the Germania, 26 August 1883. Germania's voyage
from Pentland Firth to Cumberland Sound). *Berliner
Tageblatt*, First Supplement, Sunday, 28 October 1883,
Vol. 12, No. 505:4-5.

BT 7   Dr. Fr. Boas. Im Eise des Nordens. Kikkerton, 14.
September 1883 (In the Northern Ice. Kikkerton, 14
September 1883). *Berliner Tageblatt*, First Supplement,
Sunday, 4 November 1883, Vol. 12, No. 517:4-5.

BT 8   Dr. F. Boas. Aus dem Eise des Nordens. Kikkerton, 25.
September [1883] (From the Northern Ice. Kikkerton, 25
September [1883]). *Berliner Tageblatt*, First Supplement,
Sunday, 25 November 1883, Vol. 12, No. 553:4.
*Last report sent to Berlin from Baffin Land before the ice
set in.*

BT 9   Dr. F. Boas. Kurzer Bericht über meine Reisen in
Baffinland. St. Johns, Newfoundland, 6. September 1884
(Short report on my journeys in Baffin Land. St. John's,
Newfoundland, 6 September 1884). *Berliner Tageblatt*,
First Supplement, Sunday, 28 September 1884, Vol. 13,
No. 455:2, map.
*First report after leaving Baffin Land was sent from
St. John's, Newfoundland; it includes a map of Cumberland
Sound and Davis Strait with Inuit place names drawn by
Boas.*

Articles BT 10 to 16 were sent from New York City to Berlin.

BT 10   Dr. Franz Boas. Der Walfischfang im Cumberland-Sunde
(Whaling in Cumberland Sound). *Berliner Tageblatt*,
Second Supplement, Sunday, 19 October 1884, Vol. 13,
No. 491:6-7.

BT 11   Dr. Franz Boas. Die Eskimos des Cumberland-Sundes
und der Davisstraße (The Eskimos of Cumberland Sound
and Davis Strait). *Berliner Tageblatt*, First Supplement,
Sunday, 2 November 1884, Vol. 13, No. 515:4.

Adapted translation "Cumberland Sound and its Eskimos", *Popular Science Monthly 26, April 1885:768-779.*

BT 12   Dr. Franz Boas. Reise nach Paquistu [Pangnirtung] (Trip to Pangnirtung). *Berliner Tageblatt*, First Supplement, Sunday, 9 November 1884, Vol. 13, No. 527:4-5.

BT 13   Dr. Franz Boas. Ssedna und die religiösen Herbstfeste (Ssedna and the religious fall festival). *Berliner Tageblatt*, Second Supplement, Sunday, 16 November 1884, Vol. 13, No. 539:6-7.

BT 14   Dr. Franz Boas. Der Hundeschlitten. Nordische Skizzen für das "Berliner Tageblatt" (The Dog Sled. Nordic travel sketch for the "Berliner Tageblatt"). *Berliner Tageblatt*, Second Supplement, Sunday, 23 November 1884, Vol. 13, No. 551:6-7.

BT 15   Dr. Franz Boas. Beim Gastfreunde. Nordische Reiseskizze (With the often-time host. Nordic travel sketch). *Berliner Tageblatt*, Second Supplement, Sunday, 28 December 1884, Vol. 13, No. 610:6-7.

BT 16   Dr. Franz Boas. Reise nach Anamitung [Anarnitung]. Nordische Reisebilder (Trip to Anarnitung. Nordic travel images). *Berliner Tageblatt*, Second Supplement, Sunday, 4 January 1885, Vol. 14, No. 5:6-7.

Articles BT 17 and 18 submitted in Berlin.

BT 17   Dr. Franz Boas. Aus dem hohen Norden. Reisebriefe für das "Berliner Tageblatt". Die letzten Wochen im Lande des ewigen Eises (From the Far North. Travel letters for the "Berliner Tageblatt". The last weeks in the Land of Eternal Ice). *Berliner Tageblatt*, First Supplement, Friday, 3 April 1885, Vol. 14, No. 170:4-5.

BT 18   Dr. Franz Boas. Ititaija. Eine Eskimo-Sage (Ititaija. An Eskimo Tale). *Berliner Tageblatt*, Monday, 27 April 1885, Vol. 14., No. n.d., 2 pages.
    See Boas 1887a and in particular 1888c:398-400, the complete version, and 1888e:409, 615-618 in The Central Eskimo *as Ititaujang, where Boas added the remark: "This tradition was curtailed, as some parts were considered inappropriate for publication." (1888e:616)*

1884a   A Journey in Cumberland Sound and on the West Shore of Davis Strait in 1883 and 1884. *Journal of the American Geographical Society of New York* 16:242-272, p. 241, map (also as *Bulletin of the American Geographical Society* 3, 1884:242-272, map on p. 241).
          Boas's first publication in English; reprinted in Études/Inuit/Studies *8,1, 1984:121-138 (Müller-Wille 1984).*

1884b   Brief von Dr. Franz Boas an "Globus", Alma Farm, Lake George, NY, 24. September 1884 (Letter by Dr. Franz Boas to [the magazine]"Globus", Alma Farm, Lake George, NY, 24 September 1884). *Globus* 42,22:352.
          *Also in: *Verhandlungen der Gesellschaft für Erdkunde zu Berlin 11,1884:378; letter to Adolf Bastian and Wilhelm Reiß.*

1884c   Customs of the Esquimaux. Presentation before the German Social Science [sic] Association (*Deutscher Gesellig-Wissenschaftlicher Verein von New York*) on Tuesday, November 5, 1884. *New York Times*, Wednesday, November 6, 1884:5.
          The first time that Boas was mentioned in the New York Times *upon the occasion of his first public lecture, which remained unpublished.*

1885a   Wie der Cumberland-Sund entdeckt wurde (How Cumberland Sound was discovered). *New Yorker Staats-Zeitung*, Sunday, 18 January 1885.
          English translation in Boas 2009:54-57.

1885b   Unter dem Polarkreise (Below the Arctic Circle). *New Yorker Staats-Zeitung.*
          I. (no title), Sunday, 1 February 1885;
          II. (no title), Sunday, 22 February 1885;
          III. Der Herbst (The Fall), Monday, 2 March 1885.
          English translation in Boas 2009:58-66.

1885c   Die Wohnsitze und Wanderungen der Baffinland-Eskimos (Settlements and migrations of the Baffin Land Eskimos). *Deutsche Geographische Blätter* 8:31-38, Plate 2 (map).

1885d   Bemerkungen zur Topographie der Hudsonbai und Hudsonstrasse (Remarks on the topography of Hudson

Bay and Hudson Strait). *Petermanns Geographische Mitteilungen* 31:424-426, Plate 19 (map).

1885e   Die Eskimo des Baffinlandes (The Eskimos of Baffin Land). *Verhandlungen des fünften Deutschen Geographentages zu Hamburg* am 9., 10. und 11. April 1885. Published by the Zentralausschuß des Deutschen Geographentages (Central Committee of the German Assembly of Geographers). Berlin: Dietrich Reimer, p. 101-112.

Presentation held at the Fifth German Assembly of Geographers in Hamburg on April 11, 1885. An undated and unpublished English translation "The Eskimos of Baffin Land" (16 pp.) by Ernst Boas is on file at the APS/FBFP (Zumwalt 2013b).

1885f   Die Sagen der Baffin-Land-Eskimos (The Tales of the Baffin Land Eskimos). *Verhandlungen der Berliner Gesellschaft für Anthropologie, Ethnologie und Urgeschichte* 17:161-166.

Presentation held at the Berlin Society for Anthropology, Ethnology and Prehistory on April 15, 1885; introduced by Rudolf von Virchow, President.

1885g   Reise im Baffinlande 1883 und 1884 (2. Mai 1885) (Travels in Baffin Land in 1883 and 1884 [2 May 2885]). *Verhandlungen der Gesellschaft für Erdkunde zu Berlin* 12, 5-6:288-297, map.

Presentation held in Berlin on May 2, 1885.

1885h   *Baffin-Land. Geographische Ergebnisse einer in den Jahren 1883 und 1884 ausgeführten Forschungsreise* (Baffin Land. Geographical results of a research journey conducted in the years of 1883 and 1884). Petermanns Mitteilungen, Supplementary Volume 80, 100 pp., two maps and nine sketches. Gotha: Justus Perthes. (Reprint: Saarbrücken: Bibliophiler Fines Mundus Verlag 2006, http://www.finis-mundi.de)

Boas's Habilitationsschrift in physical geography published in December 1885; the publisher apparently dropped Geographische between Petermanns and Mitteilungen for the supplementary volumes in this series.

1885i   Sammlung aus Baffin-Land (Collection from Baffin Land). *Original-Mittheilungen aus der Ethnologischen Abteilung der Königlichen Museen zu Berlin*, p. 131-133. Berlin: Verlag von W. Spemann.

Boas's annotations of his own collection of ethnographic materials from Inuit ("centralen Eskimos") in Cumberland Sound and along Davis Strait on Baffin Land in 1883-1884, with inventory numbers given.

1885j*   The Eskimo of Baffin Land. *Transactions of the Anthropological Society of Washington*, Vol. III, November 6, 1883 – May 19, 1885:95-102.

Presentation before the ASW at the Smithsonian Institution on December 2, 1884; issued in 1886, also as part of the Publication Nr. 630 of the Miscellaneous Collection of the Smithsonian Institution; *reprinted in* Études/Inuit/ Studies 8,1, 1984:139-144 *(Müller-Wille 1984).*

1885k   *Eskimoiske Sagn og Sange samlede af Dr. F. Boas paa Baffins-Land* (Eskimo tales and songs collected by Dr. F. Boas on Baffin's Land).

Handwritten and unpublished manuscript in Inuktitut and German sent by Franz Boas, Minden, to Hinrich Johann Rink, Copenhagen, April 28, 1885. 50 pp. (RLC, Rink Papers).

1885l   *Die Eisverhältnisse des arktischen Oceans* (The ice conditions of the Arctic Ocean), *Habilitationskolloquium, Philosophische Fakultät, Friedrich-Wilhelms-Universität zu Berlin*, 27 May 1885, 22 pp., handwritten, unpublished (APS/FBPP).

1885m   *Ueber das Cañongebiet des Colorado* (Concerning the Cañon Area of the Colorado), Praelectio (Inaugural Lecture), *Philosophische Fakultät, Friedrich-Wilhelms-Universität zu Berlin*, 5 June 1885, 19 pp., handwritten, unpublished (APS/FBPP).

1885n   Mr. Melville's Plan of Reaching the North Pole. *New York Evening Post*, February 6, 1885.

Letter to the Editor written by FB on February 3, 1885; George W. Melville's reply was published under the same title in the New York Evening Post, February 17, 1885.

1885o   Mr. Melville's plan of reaching the north pole. In: Letters
           to the Editor. *Science* 5, 112, March 27, 1885:247-248.
           Response by FB to Melville's letter in the New York Evening
           Post, February 17, 1885.

1885p   The Configuration of Grinnell Land and Ellesmere Island.
           Science 5, 108, February 27, 1885:170-171.

1885r   Cumberland Sound and its Eskimos. *Popular Science
           Monthly* 26, April 1885:768-779.
           Translation of the article "Die Eskimos des Cumberland-
           Sundes und der Davisstraße", *Berliner Tageblatt*, 2
           November 1884; in German Boas - *BT* 11.

1886a   Die Expedition des "Neptune" im Jahre 1884 (The "Nep-
           tune" Expedition in the Year 1884). *Deutsche Geographische
           Blätter* 9, 1:68-70.
           *Review of A. R. Gordon and Robert Bell, Report of the
           Hudson's Bay Expedition, under the command of Lieut. A.
           R. Gordon. Ottawa: s. n. (1884).*

1886b*   Litteraturbericht Nr. 234. Rink, H., Om de Eskimoiske
           Dialekter, Kjøbenhavn, 1885 (Literature Report Nr. 234,
           H. Rink, Concerning Eskimo Dialects. Copenhagen 1885).
           Petermanns Geographische Mitteilungen 32:59-60.
           Full title: Rink, Hinrich: Om de Eskimoiske Dialekter,
           som Bidrag til Bedømmelsen af Spørgsmaalet om
           Eskimoernes Herkomst og Vandringer (Concerning
           Eskimo dialects, as a contribution to the evaluation of the
           question of the origin and migrations of the Eskimos).
           Aarbøger for nordisk oldkyndighed og historie 1885:219-
           260. Kjøbenhavn: Thiele.

1887a   Religiösen Vorstellungen und einige Gebräuche der zen-
           tralen Eskimos (The religious beliefs and some customs
           of the Central Eskimos). *Petermanns Geographische
           Mitteilungen* 33, 10:302-316.

1887b   Unter den Eskimos (Among the Eskimos). *Deutsch-
           Amerikanisches Magazin. Vierteljahrsschrift für Geschichte,
           Literatur, Wissenschaft, Kunst, Schule und Volksleben der
           Deutschen in Amerika* 1:613-624. Cincinnati, Ohio: S.
           Rosenthal.
           Based closely on Boas 1885e.

1887c   A Year among the Eskimo. *Bulletin of the American Geographical Society* 19, 4:383-402.

1887-1888   Articles in **Science** on Inuit and Arctic [Sc 1-16]

Sc 1   The Study of Geography. *Science*, Friday, February 11, 1887, Supplement 9, 210:137-141.
             Reprinted as Boas 1940a:639-647; also in Agnew et al. 1996:173-180, Stocking 1996:9-16).

Sc 2   Ethnology: The Eskimo Tribes. *Science* 10, 252, December 2, 1887:271.
             Review of Hinrich J. Rink. *Eskimo Tribes.* Copenhagen: C. A. Reitzel 1887.

Sc 3   Eskimo and Indians. Response to A. F. Chamberlain's *Eskimo and Indians* (Science 10, December 2, 1887:273-274). *Science* 10, 252, December 2, 1887:274.

Sc 4   Poetry and Music of Some North American Tribes. *Science* 9, 220, April 22, 1887:383-385.
             With samples of text pieces and music scores from "Eskimos" on Baffin Land and "Indians" in British Columbia, Canada.

Sc 5   [unsigned] Eskimo Harpoon. *Science* 9, 229, June 24, 1887:607-608, one figure.

Sc 6   [unsigned] The Exploration of Arctic America. *Science* 10, 230, July 1, 1887:3-4.

Sc 7   [unsigned] Exploration and Travel. Notes from the Arctic. *Science* 10, 249, November 11, 1887:233-234, map.

Sc 8   [unsigned] The New Route from England to Asia, and the Hudson Bay Route. *Science* 10, 231, July 8, 1887:15-17, map.

Sc 9   Ice and Icebergs. *Science* 9, 217, April 1, 1887:324-325.

Sc 10   The Formation and Dissipation of Sea-Water Ice. *Science* 10, 239, September 2, 1887:118-119.

Sc 11   Response to A. F. Chamberlain's *Vermin-Eaters* (*Science* 11, 265, March 2, 1888:109). *Science* 11, March 2, 1888:109.

Sc 12   [F. B.] An Ethnographical Collection from Alaska. *Science* 11, 273, April 27, 1888:198-199.

Sc 13   [unsigned] Yukon Expedition, 1887. *Science* 11, 272, April 20, 1888:184-185, map.

Sc 14   [unsigned] Exploration in Greenland. *Science* 11, 278, June 1, 1888:259-260, map.

Sc 15   [unsigned] Notes on the Geography of Labrador. *Science* 11, 263, February 17, 1888:77-79, two maps.

Sc 16   [unsigned] The Great Mackenzie Basin. *Science* 11, 307, December 21, 1888:314-15, two maps.

1888a   Die Eisverhältnisse des südöstlichen Teiles von Baffin-Land (The ice conditions in the southeastern part of Baffin Land). *Petermanns Geographische Mitteilungen* 34:296-298, map.

1888b   Das Fadenspiel (The Game of Cat's Cradle). *Mittheilungen der Anthropologischen Gesellschaft in Wien* 18 (N. F. 8), 7: 85.
See also Boas 1888f.

1888c   Sagen der Eskimos von Baffin-Land (Eskimo tales from Baffin Land). *Verhandlungen der Berliner Gesellschaft für Anthropologie, Ethnologie und Urgeschichte* 20:398-405.

1888d   Meteorologische Beobachtungen im Cumberland-Sunde (Meteorological observations in Cumberland Sound). *Annalen der Hydrographie und maritimen Meteorologie* 16, 6:241-262.

1888e   *The Central Eskimo.* Sixth Annual Report of the Bureau of Ethnology 1884-85 [1888]: 399-669, Fig. No. 390-546, Plates II-X. Washington: Smithsonian Institution. *Reprint:* Introduction by Henry B. Collins. Lincoln: Bison Book, University of Nebraska Press 1964; *facsimile reprint:* Coles Canadiana Collection. Toronto: Coles Publishing Company Limited 1974.

1888f   The Game of Cat's Cradle. *Internationales Archiv für Ethnographie* 1, 1888:229-230, 5 illustrations, and 2, 1889:52.

1888g   [Franz Boaz (*sic*)] The Tribal Division of the Eskimos of Northeastern America. *American Antiquarian and Oriental Journal* 10:40-41.

1888h   The Eskimo. *Transactions of the Royal Society of Canada for the Year* 1887, 5, 2:35-39.

1888i   The Geography and Geology of Baffin Land. *Transactions of the Royal Society of Canada* for the Year 1887, 5, 2:75-78.

1894a   Der Eskimo-Dialekt des Cumberland-Sundes (The Eskimo dialect of Cumberland Sound). *Mittheilungen der Anthropologischen Gesellschaft in Wien* 24 (Neue Folge 14):97-114.

1894b   Eskimo Tales and Songs. *Journal of American Folk-Lore* 7:45-50.

1894c   Notes on the Eskimo of Port Clarence, Alaska. *Journal of American Folk-Lore* 7:205-208.

1897   Eskimo Tales and Songs. *Journal of American Folk-Lore* 10:109-115.

1899   Property Marks of Alaskan Eskimo. *American Anthropologist, New Series*, 1, 4:601-613, 10 figures.

1900   Religious Beliefs of the Central Eskimo. *Popular Science Monthly* 57, October 1900:624-631.

1901   The Eskimo of the Baffin Land and Hudson Bay: from notes collected by George Comer, James S. Mutch, and E. J. [Edmund James] Peck. *Bulletin of the American Museum of Natural History* 15, Part I:1-370. New York: Published by the order of the Trustees, American Museum of Natural History (see Part II: Boas 1907).
            Reprint: New York: AMS Press 1975.

1903   The Eskimo Collection from Hudson Bay. *The American Museum Journal* 3:6-9, map.

1904   The Folk-Lore of the Eskimos. *Journal of American Folk-Lore* 17:1-13.

1906   The Eskimo. *Annual Archaeological Report* 1905, being part of the Appendix to the *Report of the Minister of Education, Ontario Legislative Assembly*. Toronto: L. K. Cameron, p. 107-116.

1907   Second Report on the Eskimo of the Baffin Land and Hudson Bay: from notes collected by Captain George Comer, Captain James S. Mutch, and Rev[erend]. E. J.

[Edmund James] Peck. *Bulletin of the American Museum of Natural History* 15, Part II:371-570. New York: Published by the order of the Trustees, American Museum of Natural History (see Part I: Boas 1901) *Reprint*: New York: AMS Press 1975.

1908a   Decorative Designs of Alaskan Needlecases: A Study in the History of Conventional Designs, Based on Materials in the United States National Museum. *Proceedings of the United States National Museum* 34, 1908:321-344, 9 plates, 16 illustrations. Washington: Smithsonian Institution. *Reprint*: Boas 1940a:546-563.

1908b   Bird-Bolas among the Eastern Eskimo. *American Anthropologist, New Series*, 10, 4:698-699.

1909a   Needle-Case from Grinnell Land. *American Anthropologist, New Series*, 11:135-136.

1909b   Review of Rasmussen's *The People of the Polar North*. *Journal of American Folk-Lore* 22:264. *Complete title*: *The People of the Polar North: A Record*. By Knud Rasmussen, G. Herring, and Count Harald Moltke. Philadelphia, Pennsylvania: J. B. Lippincott & Co. 1908.

1909c   Relationships of the Eskimos of East Greenland. *Science* 30, 772, October 15, 1909:535-536. *Reprint*: Boas 1940a: 593-595.

1922*   An Eskimo Winter. In: Parsons, Elsie Clews (ed.), *American Indian Life by Several of Its Students*. Illustrated by C. Grant La Farge. New York: B. W. Huebsch, p.367-378, 413. *First of several reprints*: New York: The Viking Press 1925. *The story about life in winter with two chants related by Pakkak, one of Boas's Inuit experts on place names and tales on Baffin Land.*

1926   Two Eskimo Riddles from Labrador. *Journal of American Folk-Lore* 39 [1927]:486.

1932   *Rasse und Kultur*. Rede, gehalten am 30ten Juli 1931 in der Aula der Christian-Albrechts-Universität in Kiel bei Gelegenheit des 50jährigen Doktorsjubiläums des

Verfassers (Race and Culture. Presentation held at the occasion of the author's 50th doctoral anniversary in the auditorium of the *Christian-Albrechts-Universität* at Kiel on July 30, 1931). Jena: Verlag von Gustav Fischer. 19 pp. *Reprinted in* Zeitschrift für Kulturphilosophie 6, 2, 2012:377-390. Hamburg: Felix Meiner Verlag; *Pöhl 2012.*

1933a   *Offener Brief.* Seine Exzellenz Generalfeldmarschall Paul von Hindenburg, Präsident des Deutschen Reiches, Berlin, Germany. Franz Boas, Columbia University, New York City, den 27. März 1933. 4 pp. (APS/FBPP).

See also Sundergeld 1980:185-188, a 450th anniversary volume of FB's high school in Minden, in which, along with a short biography of FB, his Open Letter was published the first time in Germany almost 50 years after its clandestine distribution at the beginning of the Third Reich; also reprinted in Rodekamp 1994:94-95.

1933b   Arier und Nicht-Arier (Aryans and Non-Aryans). *Die Neue Welt.* Deutschsprachiges Tagesorgan der Kommunistischen Partei Frankreichs, Region Elsaß-Lothringen (New World, German Daily of the Communist Party of France, Alsace-Lorraine Region) 10, 257-259, November 6, 7 and 8, 1933. Straßburg.

German translation of the original English manuscript written in 1933 and published later with some revisions as Boas 1934a.

1934a   Aryans and Non-Aryans. *The American Mercury,* June 1934, 32, 116:219-223.

1934b   *Geographical Names of the Kwakiutl Indians.* Columbia University Contributions to Anthropology 20. New York: Columbia University Press.

Extensive survey of geographical places with explanations and translations (83 pages) and an atlas of 22 maps; it includes Boas's comparison of "Kwakiutl and Eskimo nomenclature" *(p. 18-19).*

1940a   *Race, Language and Culture.* New York: The Macmillan Company.

Compendium of Franz Boas's selected publications.

1940b   Liberty among Primitive People. In: *Freedom, Its Meaning.* Planned and edited by Ruth Nanda Anshen. New York: Harcourt, Brace and Company, p. 375-380. *With contributions by forty-three writers; reissued:* London: G. Allen & Unwin 1942.

Posthumous publications:

2007   *Eskimo Story (Written for my Children). My Arctic Expedition.* Edited by Norman F. Boas. Mystic, Connecticut: Seaport Autographs Press.

2009   *Arctic Expedition 1883-1884.* Translated German Newspaper Accounts of My Life with the Eskimos. Edited by Norman F. Boas and Doris W. Boas. Translated by Rita Terris and Thomas Huber. Mystic, CT: Norman F. Boas. Private edition.

      Newspaper articles by Franz Boas published in the Berliner Tageblatt *between 1883 and 1885 (above as BT 3-18) and in the* New Yorker Staats-Zeitung *in 1885 (above as Boas 1885a-b).*

References

Abbes, Heinrich

1884   Die Eskimos des Cumberland-Sundes. Eine ethnographische Skizze (The Eskimos of Cumberland Sound. An ethnographic sketch). *Globus* 46:198-201, 213-218.

1890   Die Eskimos des Cumberlandgolfes (The Eskimos of the Golf of Cumberland). In: Neumayer, Georg von (ed.), *Die internationale Polarforschung 1882-1883.* Die Deutschen Expeditionen und ihre Ergebnisse. Band II: Beschreibende Naturwissenschaften in einzelnen Abhandlungen. (International Polar Research 1882-1883. The German Expeditions and Their Results. Volume II: Descriptive Natural Sciences in Individual Treatises.) Hamburg: Deutsche Polar-Kommission, p. 1-60.

Agnew, John & David J. Livingstone, Alisdair Rogers (eds)

1996   *Human Geography. An Essential Anthology.* New York: John Wiley & Sons.

Ambronn, Leopold [L. A.]

1883   Bemerkungen über den Cumberland-Sund und seine
             Bewohner (Comments about Cumberland Sound and its
             inhabitants). *Deutsche Geographische Blätter* 6:347-357.

Andrews, H. A.

1906   Bibliography of Franz Boas. In: Laufer 1906:515-545.
             FB's publications from 1880 to 1906.

Andrews, H. A. and others

1943   Bibliography of Franz Boas. Edited by Bertha C. Edel. In:
             Kroeber, Alfred L., ed., Franz Boas 1858-1942. *American
             Anthropological Association Memoirs* 61:67-119.
             FB's publications from 1880 to 1943.

Bender-Wittmann, Ursula

2007   Zwischen den Welten. Aspekte von Identität und Mobilität
             im Werdegang von Franz Boas (1858-1942) (Between
             worlds. Aspects of identity and mobility in the career of
             Franz Boas (1858-1942)). *Lippische Mitteilungen aus
             Geschichte und Landeskunde* 76:103-127.

Boas, Norman F.

2004   *Franz Boas 1858-1942. An Illustrated Biography.* Mystic,
             CT: Seaport Autograph Press.

Boas, Norman Francis & Barbara Linton Meyer

1999   *Alma Farm. An Adirondack Meeting Place.* Mystic,
             Connecticut & Bolton Landing, New York: Boas & Meyer
             Publishers.

Brilling, Bernhard

1966   Die Vorfahren des Professors Franz Boas (Ancestors of
             Professor Franz Boas). *Mindener Heimatblätter, Mittei-
             lungsblatt des Mindener Geschichts- und Museumsverein*
             1966,3-4:1-2. Special Supplement to *Mindener Tageblatt*,
             24 April 1966 (also in: *Mitteilungen des Mindener Geschichts-
             und Museumsvereins* 38:103-112).

Broce, Gerald L.

1973   History of Anthropology. Basic Concepts in Anthropology.
        Edited by A. J. (Jack) Kelso and Aram Yengoyan.
        Minneapolis, Minnesota: Burgess Publishing Company.

1986   Herder and Ethnography. Journal of the History of the
        Behavioral Sciences 22:150-170.

Bunzl, Matti

1996   Franz Boas and the Humboldtian Tradition: From
        Volksgeist and Nationalcharakter to an Anthropological
        Concept of Culture. In: Stocking 1996:17-78.

Cole, Douglas

1983   "The Value of a Person Lies in his Herzensbildung". Franz
        Boas' Baffin Island Letter-Diary, 1883-1884. In: Stocking
        Jr., George W. (ed.), Observers Observed. Essays on
        Ethnographic Fieldwork. History of Anthropology, Vol. 1.
        Madison: University of Wisconsin Press, p. 13-52.

1999   Franz Boas. The Early Years, 1858-1906. Vancouver/
        Toronto: Douglas & McIntyre, Seattle/London: University
        of Washington Press.

Cole, Douglas & Ludger Müller-Wille

1984   Franz Boas' Expedition to Baffin Island, 1883-1884. Études/
        Inuit/Studies 8,1:37-63.

Dorais, Louis-Jacques

1996   La parole inuit. Langue, culture et société dans l'Arctique
        nord-américain. Société d'Études Linguistiques et
        Anthropologiques de France - Selaf No. 347, Collection
        Arctique 3. Paris: Peters.

Dürr, Michael & Erich Kasten, Egon Renner (eds)

1992   Franz Boas. Ethnologe - Anthropologe - Spachwissens-
        chaftler. Ein Wegbereiter der modernen Wissenschaft vom
        Menschen. (Franz Boas. Ethnologist - Anthropologist -
        Linguist. A trailblazer of the modern science of human-
        kind). Berlin: Staatsbibliothek - Preußischer Kulturbesitz.

Espagne, Michel & Isabelle Kalinoskwi (eds)

2013   *Franz Boas. Le travail du regard.* Paris: Éditions Armand Colin.

Études/Inuit/Studies

1977   Projet de conférence inuit / Proposed Inuit Conference. *Études/Inuit/Studies* 1, 1:170-171.

Fallon, Daniel

1976   *The German University. A Heroic Ideal in Conflict with the Modern World.* Boulder. CO: Colorado Associated University Press.

Freeman, Milton M. R. (ed.)

1984   Dans les traces de Boas - 100 ans d'anthropologie des Inuit – In Boas' Footsteps - 100 Years of Inuit Anthropology. *Études/Inuit/Studies* 8,1:3-179.

Guttridge, Leonard F.

2000   *Ghosts of Cape Sabine. The Harrowing True Story of the Greely Expedition.* New York: Berkley Books.

Harper, Kenn

2000   *Give me my father's body. The life of Minik, the New York Eskimo.* South Royalton, VT: Steerforth Press and New York: Washington Square Press. (Original edition: Frobisher Bay, N.W.T. [Iqaluit, Nunavut]: Blacklead Books, 1986).

2008   The collaboration of James Mutch and Franz Boas, 1883-1922. In: Müller-Wille, ed. 2008:53-71.

Jewish Encyclopedia

1906   Tisza-Eszlar Affair. In: *Jewish Encyclopedia.* New York: Funk & Wagnalls 1901-1906. http://www.jewishencyclopedia.com/articles/14407-tisza-eszlar-affair (accessed January 23, 2013).

Knötsch, Carol Cathleen

1988   *Franz Boas bei den kanadischen Inuit im Jahre 1883-1884* (Franz Boas among the Canadian Inuit in the Year 1883-1884). Master's thesis, Ethnology, *Rheinische Friedrich-*

Wilhelms-Universität, Bonn, Germany. (Published: *Mundus Reihe Ethnologie* 60. Bonn: Holos Verlag 1992.)

Kroeber, Alfred L.

1899   The Eskimo of Smith Sound. *Bulletin of the American Museum of Natural History* 12:265-327.

1901   Decorative Symbolism of the Arapaho. *American Anthropologist, New Series* 3:308-336.

Krupnik, Igor (ed.)

2014   *Early Inuit Studies. Themes and Profiles in Eskimology, 1850-1980s.* Washington, DC: Smithsonian Institution Scholarly Press.

Krupnik, Igor & Ludger·Müller-Wille

2010   Franz Boas and Inuktitut Terminology for Ice and Snow: From the Emergence of the Field to the "Great Eskimo Vocabulary Hoax". In: Krupnik, Igor & Claudio Aporta, Shari Gearheard, Gita J. Laidler, Lene Kielsen Holm (eds), *SIKU: Knowing Our Ice. Documenting Inuit Sea-Ice Knowledge and Use.* Dordrecht, Heidelberg, London, New York: Springer Verlag, p. 377-400.

Krupnik, Igor & Ludger Müller-Wille (eds)

2010   The Beginnings of Arctic Social Sciences: Reconstructing the Genealogy of IASSA. Special Issue Celebrating the 20th Anniversary of IASSA and Honoring Ernest S. Burch, Jr. (1938-2010). *Northern Notes - Newsletter of the International Arctic Social Sciences Association* 33, Anniversary Issue. Akureyri: IASSA Secretariat. http://www.iassa.org/images/stories/newsletters/northern_notes_33_anniversary_issue_2010.pdf

Kumlien, Ludwig (ed.)

1879   *Contributions to the Natural History of Arctic America, made in connection with the Howgate Polar Expedition, 1877-78.* Department of the Interior, Bulletin of the United States National Museum 15. Washington: Smithsonian Institution.

Langenkämper, Jürgen

2009   *"Ich fuerchte nur, wir verstehen einander nicht".* Franz
            Boas' Briefwechsel mit deutschen Freunden und Kollegen
            1932/33 ("I just fear that we do not understand each other."
            Franz Boas's correspondence with German friends and
            colleagues). In: Pöhl, Friedrich & Bernhard Tilg (eds),
            *Franz Boas. Kultur, Sprache, Rasse. Wege einer antiras-
            sistischen Anthropologie.* Wien: Lit Verlag, p. 131-149.

Laufer, Berthold (ed.)

1906   *Boas Anniversary Volume. Anthropological Papers Written
            in Honor of Franz Boas.* Presented to him on the twenty-
            fifth anniversary of his doctorate, ninth of August, nine-
            teen hundred and six. New York: G. E. Stechert & Co.

Lévi-Strauss, Claude

1984   Claude Lévi-Strauss' Testimony on Franz Boas. *Études/
            Inuit/Studies* 8,1:7-9.

Lewis, Herbert S.

2001   The Passion of Franz Boas. *American Anthropologist*
            103,2:447-467.

2008   Franz Boas: Boon or Bane? *Reviews in Anthropology*
            37:169-200.

Liss, Julia E.

1995   Patterns of Strangeness. Franz Boas, Modernism, and the
            Origins of Anthropology. In: Barkan, Elazar & Ronald
            Bush (eds), *Prehistories of the Future. The Primitivist
            Project and the Culture of Modernism.* Stanford: Stanford
            University Press, p. 114-130.

1996   German Culture and German Science in the *Bildung* of
            Franz Boas. In: Stocking 1996:155-184.

Lowie, Robert H.

1947   Biographical Memoir of Franz Boas 1858-1942. Presented
            to the Academy at the Annual Meeting, 1947. *National
            Academy of Sciences of the United States of America,
            Biographical Memoirs* 24:303-322.

Mathewson, Kent

2002   Review of William W. Speth, How it came to be: Carl O.
            Sauer, Franz Boas, and the Meaning of Anthropogeography.
            Ellensberg, WA: Ephemera Press 1999. *American Anthro-
            pologist* 104,1:380-381.

Mommsen, Theodor

1880   *Auch ein Wort über unser Judentum* (Even another Word
            about Our Judaism). Berlin: Weidmannsche Buchhand-
            lung.

Müller-Wille, Ludger

1983   Franz Boas (1858-1942). Arctic Profiles. *Arctic* 36,2:
            212-213.

1984   Two Papers by Franz Boas. *Études/Inuit/Studies* 8,1:
            117-144.
            See Boas 1884a and 1885j.

1994   Franz Boas und seine Forschungen bei den Inuit. Der
            Beginn einer arktischen Ethnologie (Franz Boas and his
            research among Inuit. The beginning of Arctic eth-
            nology). In: Rodekamp 1994:25-38.

2014   Franz Boas: His English Language Publications on Inuit
            and the Arctic (1884-1926) and Critical Assessments since
            the Early 1980s. A Bibliographical Survey. In: Krupnik
            2014.

Müller-Wille, Ludger (ed.)

1992   Franz Boas: Auszüge aus seinem Baffin-Tagebuch 1883-
            1884 (10. September bis 15. Oktober 1883) (Franz Boas:
            Excerpts from his Baffin Diary 1883-1884 (September 10
            to October 15, 1883). In: Dürr 1992:39-56.

1994   *Franz Boas. Bei den Inuit in Baffinland 1883-1884. Tage-
            bücher und Briefe* (Franz Boas. Among the Inuit on Baffin
            Land 1883-1884. Journals and letters). Ethnologische
            Beiträge zur Circumpolarforschung 1, Editor: Erich
            Kasten. Berlin: Reinhold Schletzer Verlag.
            Original source: Boas 1882-1884.

1998   *Franz Boas among the Inuit of Baffin Island 1883-1884.*
            Journals and Letters. Translated by William Barr. Toronto,
            Buffalo, London: University of Toronto Press.
            Original source: Boas 1882-1884.

2008   Franz Boas et les Inuit / Franz Boas and the Inuit. *Études/*
            Inuit/Studies 32,2:5-84.
            With an introduction by Ludger Müller-Wille - Franz Boas
            et les Inuit (p 5-8), Franz Boas and the Inuit (p 9-12).

Müller-Wille, Ludger & Bernd Gieseking (eds)

2008   *Bei Inuit und Walfängern auf Baffin-Land (1883/1884). Das*
            arktische Tagebuch des Wilhelm Weike (Among Inuit and
            Whalers in Baffin Land (1883/1884). Wilhelm Weike's
            Arctic journal). Mindener Beiträge 30. Minden: Mindener
            Geschichtsverein.
            Original source: Weike 1883-1889.

Müller-Wille, Ludger & Bernd Gieseking

2011   *Inuit and Whalers on Baffin Island through German Eyes.*
            Wilhelm Weike's Arctic Journal and Letters (1883-84).
            Translated by William Barr. Montréal: Baraka Books.
            Original source: Weike 1883-1889.

Müller-Wille, Ludger & Linna Weber Müller-Wille

2006   Inuit Geographical Knowledge One Hundred Years Apart.
            In: Stern, Pamela & Lisa Stevenson (eds), *Critical Inuit*
            Studies. An Anthology of Contemporary Arctic Ethno-
            graphy. Lincoln and London: University of Nebraska
            Press, p. 217-229.

Mutch, James S.

1906   Whaling in Ponds Bay. In: Laufer 1906:485-500.

Pilling, James C.

1887   *Bibliography of the Eskimo Language.* Bureau of Ethnology
            Bulletin 1. Washington: Bureau of Ethnology, Smithsonian
            Institution, Government Printing Office.

Pöhl, Friedrich

2008   Assessing Franz Boas' ethics in his Arctic and later anthro-
            pological fieldwork. In: Müller-Wille, ed. 2008:35-52.

2012   Franz Boas' Rede an der Universität Kiel zum 50jährigen
            Doktorjubiläum (Franz Boas's speech at Kiel University
            at the occasion of the fiftieth doctoral anniversary).
            Zeitschrift für Kulurphilosophie 6,2:391-397.

2013   *Personal communications.* March-April 2013. Lecturer,
            Leopold-Franzens-Universität Innsbruck, Austria.

Ratzel, Friedrich

1882   *Anthropo-Geographie oder Grundzüge der Anwendung
            der Erdkunde auf die Geschichte* (Anthropo-Geography
            or Fundamental Features for the Application of Geogra-
            phy to History). Stuttgart: Engelhorn.

1883   Die Bedeutung der Polarforschung für die Geographie
            (The Importance of polar research for geography).
            *Verhandlungen des dritten Deutschen Geographentages zu
            Frankfurt a. M., 29., 30. und 31. März 1883.* Berlin: Dietrich
            Reimer, p. 21-37.

1887   Die amerikanischen Hyperboröer. (The American Hyper-
            boreans.) In: *Völkerkunde*, Band 2: Die Naturvölker
            Ozeaniens, Amerikas und Asiens. Die Naturvölker der
            Polarländer (Ethnology, Vol. 2: The Primitive Peoples of
            Oceania, the Americas, and Asia. The Primitive Peoples of
            the Polar Countries). Leipzig: Verlag des Bibliographischen
            Institutes, p. 732-753.

Rink, Hinrich

1890   Litteraturbericht 1132. Boas, F.: The Central Eskimo. (Ann.
            Rep. Bureau of Ethnology, Washington 1888, S. 399-669,
            mit 9 Tafeln.) *Petermanns Geographische Mitteilungen*
            36:82-83.

Rink, Hinrich & Franz Boas

1889   Eskimo Tales and Songs. *Journal of American Folk-Lore*
            2:123-131.
            *Original texts and music scores; see also under Publications
            by Franz Boas.*

Rodekamp, Volker (ed.)

1994   *Franz Boas 1858-1942. Ein amerikanischer Anthropologe
            aus Minden* (Franz Boas 1858-1942. An American anthro-

pologist from Minden). Texte und Materialien aus dem Mindener Museum 11. Bielefeld: Verlag für Regionalgeschichte.

Saladin d'Anglure, Bernard

1984   Les masques de Boas. Franz Boas et l'ethnographie des Inuit. *Études/Inuit/Studies* 8, 1:165-179.

Schott, Rüdiger

1994   Kultur und Sprache. Franz Boas als Begründer der anthropologischen Linguistik (Culture and Language. Franz Boas as founder of anthropological linguistics). In: Rodekamp 1994:25-38.

Speth, William W.

1978   The Anthropogeographic Theory of Franz Boas. *Anthropos* 73,1-2:1-31.

1999   *How it came to be. Carl O. Sauer, Franz Boas, and the Meaning of Anthropogeography.* Ellensberg, WA: Ephemera Press.
            Review by Mathewson 2002.

Spink, John & D. W. Moodie

1972   *Eskimo Maps from the Canadian Eastern Arctic.* Cartographica, Monograph 5. Toronto: Department of Geography, York University.

Stocking Jr., George W.

1965   From Physics to Ethnology: Franz Boas' Arctic Expedition as a Problem in the Historiography of the Behavioral Sciences. *Journal of the History of the Behavioral Sciences* 1:53-66.

Stocking Jr., George W. (ed.)

1996   Volksgeist *as Method and Ethic. Essays on Boasian Ethnography and the German Anthropological Tradition.* History of Anthropology 8. Madison, WI: The University of Wisconsin Press.

Stöcker, Adolf

1885   Das Judentum im öffentlichen Leben ist eine Gefahr für
            das Deutsche Reich. Rede, gehalten auf einer Christlich-
            Sozialen Parteiversammlung in Berlin, 3. 2. 1882 (Judaism
            in Public Life is a Danger to the German Reich. Speech
            held at an assembly of the Christian Social Party in Berlin
            on February 3, 1882). In: Stöcker, Alfred. *Christlich-Sozial:
            Reden und Aufsätze* (Christian Social. Speeches and
            Articles). Bielefeld, Leipzig: Velhagen & Klasing 1885.

Sundergeld, Friedhelm (ed.)

1980   *Land und Leuten dienen. Ein Lesebuch zur Geschichte der
            Schule in Minden zum 450jährigen Bestehen im Auftrag
            des Ratsgymnasiums Minden* (To serve country and
            people. A reader of Minden's school history commis-
            sioned by the Ratsgymnasium at the 450th anniversary of
            its existence). Minden: Ratsgymnasium der Stadt Minden.

Treitschke, Heinrich von

1879   Judenfrage (Jewish Question). *Preußische Jahrbücher*
            44:572-575.

Ulrikab, Abraham

2005   *The Diary of Abraham Ulrikab. Text and Content.*
            Translated from the German by Hartmut Lutz and stu-
            dents of the University of Greifswald. Ottawa: University
            of Ottawa Press.

Verne, Markus

2004   Promotion, Expedition, Habilitation, Emigration. Franz
            Boas und der schwierige Prozeß, ein wissenschaftliches
            Leben zu planen (Doctorate, expedition, habilitation,
            emigration. Franz Boas and the arduous process to plan
            a scientific existence). *Paideuma* 50:79-99.

Weike, Wilhelm

1883-1889   Hand-written journal and letters, Germany - Baffin Land
            - Germany, June 10, 1883 – January 21, 1889 (APS/FBFP).
            *Published in German in Müller-Wille & Gieseking, eds.
            2008:18-218 and in English in Müller-Wille & Gieseking
            2011:26-212.*

Wenzel, George

1984   L'écologie culturelle et les Inuit du Canada. Une approche appliquée. *Études/Inuit/Studies* 8,1:89-101.

Willis Jr., William S.

1972   Skeletons in the Anthropological Closet. In: Hymes, Dell (ed.), *Reinventing Anthropology*. New York: Vintage Books, Random House, p. 121-152.

Zumwalt, Rosemary Lévy

1982   The Sea Spirit of the Central Eskimo and Her Relationship to the Living: A Delicate Balance. *Actes des Journées d'Études en Litterature Orale*, Analyse des contes - Problèmes de méthodes, Paris, 23-26 mars 1982. Geneviève Calame-Griaule et al. (eds). Colloques Internationaux de CNRS [Centre national de la recherche scientifique]. Paris: Éditions du CNRS, p. 277-293.

1988   *American Folklore Scholarship. A Dialogue of Dissent.* Bloomington and Indianapolis: Indiana University Press.

2012   The Shaping of Intellectual Identity and Discipline through Charismatic Leaders: Franz Boas and Alan Dundes. *Western Folklore* 72, 2:131-179.

2013a   *Franz Boas. A Love Story.* Unpublished biography quoted with permission by the author.

2013b   *Personal communications.* Dean of the College Emerita and Professor Emerita of Anthropology, Agnes Scott College, Decatur, Georgia, U. S. A.

Zumwalt, Rosemary Lévy & William Shedrick Willis, Jr.

2008   *Franz Boas and W. E. B. Du Bois at Atlanta University 1906.* Transactions of the American Philosophical Society 96, 2. Philadelphia, PA: American Philosophical Society.

Index

Inuit and Whalers on Baffin Island Through German Eyes
Wilhelm Weike's Arctic Journal and Letters (1883-84)
Ludger Müller-Wille & Bernd Gieseking (trans. William Barr)

Joseph-Elzéar Bernier
Champion of Canadian Arctic Sovereignty
Marjolaine Saint-Pierre (trans. William Barr)

America's Gift
What the World Owes to the Americas and Their First Inhabitants
Käthe Roth and Denis Vaugeois

Challenging the Mississippi Firebombers
Memories of Mississippi 1964-65
Jim Dann

The First Jews in North America
The Extraordinary Story of the Hart Family
Denis Vaugeois

Slouching Towards Sirte
NATO's War on Libya and Africa
Maximilian Forte

Rwanda and the New Scramble for Africa
From Tragedy to Useful Imperial Fiction
Robin Philpot

Barack Obama and the Jim Crow Media
The Return of the Nigger Breakers
Ishmael Reed

Going Too Far
Essays about America's Nervous Breakdown
Ishmael Reed

The Question of Separatism
Quebec and the Struggle over Sovereignty
Jane Jacobs